SIMPLE SIMULATIONS II:
A Collection of Simulation/Games for Political Scientists

Edited by Charles Walcott
University of Minnesota

AMERICAN POLITICAL SCIENCE ASSOCIATION
1527 New Hampshire Avenue, N.W.
Washington, D.C. 20036

The preparation of *Simple Simulations II* is a result of two projects on behalf of the continuing education of political science faculty:

- The Professional Development Program initiated with a grant from the Fund for Post-Secondary Education. The grant supported a program of short courses on learning theories and teaching techniques in June 1976 and August 1977.

- The Professional Development Program sustained with a grant from the Lilly Endowment. The grant supported the efforts by alumni of the summer short course program to organize and direct comparable teaching short courses and workshops for colleagues in conjunction with the annual meetings of state and regional associations.

This monograph has been developed by participants in the short course on simulations in the Professional Development Program. The monograph has been approved for publication by the Committee on Educational Policy and Programs. However, the views expressed are those of the author and contributors and not those of the Committee on Educational Policy and Programs or of the American Political Science Association.

Table of Contents

Preface v

I. The Simple Simulation 1

II. The Objectives of Simulation 7

III. The Simulations 14

   A. General American Politics

      1. Anne Walcott and Ann Wynia, "Politics and the
         Policy-Making Process" 14
      2. Robert E. Eagle, "Congress Decides" 24
      3. Marie Natoli, "Chief" 36
      4. Louis E. Leopold, "Crisis Decision-Making:
         The World from Washington" 41

   B. Public Administration

      1. Dennis J. O'Donnell, Peter H. Koehn, and Robert E. Eagle,
         "Collective Bargaining in Higher Education" 43

   C. Judicial Process

      1. Thomas R. Hensley, "Krause v. Rhodes:
         The Kent State Civil Trial" 58

   D. State and Local Government

      1. William C. Johnson, "Frogtown: A Simulation of
         Urban Politics" 73
      2. Russell Brooker, "Budget-Making" 81
      3. Russell Brooker, "Slate-Making" 87
      4. Ann Wynia and Anne Walcott, "Precinct Caucus" 91

   E. Political Theory

      1. Roberta Ann Johnson, "The Aristotle Game" 98
      2. James A. Blessing, "Zorax" 102

   F. Comparative Politics

      1. Gary W. Wynia, "Latin American Nation-State" 104
      2. Peter H. Koehn and Robert E. Eagle, "African Nation" 111
      3. Louis E. Leopold, "The Parliamentary Game" 114
      4. JoAnn F. Aviel, "Forging Economic Development Policy
         in Third World Countries" 117

   G. International Politics

      1. Lewis Brownstein, "The Geneva Conference on the
         Middle East" 120

  2. Ralph M. Goldman, "World Security and Disarmament
     Conference" 129
  3. Seth Thompson, "World Disarmament Conference" 132
  4. JoAnn F. Aviel, "Conference Diplomacy" 144
  5. J. E. Lawyer, "Three International Politics Simulations" 146

H. Political Structure, Behavior, and Analysis
  1. Donald Ostrom, "Who Gets What, When and How?" 149
  2. Seth Thompson, "Exercises in Tacit Coordination" 154
  3. Roberta Ann Johnson, "Identifying Variables". 157

Preface

This volume is a follow-up to an earlier effort, *Simple Simulations*.[1] The focus of that monograph was upon the analysis of simulations—it sought to help equip the reader to evaluate simulations critically, as well as to construct original games. As a result, it contained a great deal of discussion of simulation in general, but not much attention to any simulation in particular. While the monograph was generally well-received, one constructive criticism was recurrent: it would have been helpful to have had more, and more extensive, examples.

In what follows, an attempt is made to respond to that criticism. Fortunately, since 1976 I have offered, under the *aegis* of the APSA, a short course on Simple Simulations. This has brought me into contact with a stimulating variety of political scientists with strong interests in simulation. Thus I was able to ask these colleagues, along with others who came to my attention, to contribute reasonably brief descriptions of their own original simulations to this volume. That it turned out to be relatively easy in this way to assemble a collection that covers most of the discipline attests both to the fact that simulation is a versatile teaching tool and to the fact that a lot of political scientists are not only using, but designing their own games.

I asked the contributors represented herein to describe their simulations in enough detail that a colleague could, without difficulty, adopt them directly. This is perhaps a partial retreat from the position, taken in the earlier monograph, that instructors would be best off designing their own games. But I realize now, more clearly than I did then, that many people who are relatively unfamiliar with simulation simply don't feel confident enough with the technique to employ games of their own design. Moreover, with many ingenious designers hard at work producing games already, it seems only reasonable that others would wish to avail themselves of their products. Still, I would urge instructors to consider doing what many would probably do without any urging at all: adapt these games to your own style and approach, and to the aptitudes and needs of your students. Indeed, many of the simulations portrayed here have themselves evolved since being written up. Simulation rules are always written on paper, never in stone.

While I have tried, to some extent, to standardize the content of these descriptions, I have not prescribed a particular format. Thus some simulations are written up in something like outline form, while others are more elegantly

---

[1]Charles Walcott with Anne Walcott, *Simple Simulations: A Guide to the Design and Use of Simulation/Games in Teaching Political Science*. Washington, D.C.: American Political Science Association, 1976.

narrated. Some, moreover, include game forms, evaluation instruments and other supplementary materials, while others are more sparsely described. The reader is urged to examine each contribution, most definitely including those outside her or his substantive area, since not only such supplementary materials, but central organizing ideas may be transferable from one content area to another. None of the games included here is redundant; each has at least an idea or a twist not to be found in any of the others. Even where superficial resemblances seem overwhelming (all of the International Politics entries seem to be about conferences, for instance), each simulation proves to be different from the others, and serves to demonstrate yet another option available to the designer or adapter.

As an aid to analysis of the foregoing sort—and because our original monograph is now out of print—two sections from the first *Simple Simulations* have been reproduced here. If I were to rewrite them, I wouldn't change them much, though what we labeled a "legislative" type simulation should almost certainly be called something else. I hope not only that this material proves helpful in sorting out the simulations themselves, but that the simulation descriptions will give additional meaning to the relatively abstract discussion of the nature of the beast.

As always, a number of people deserve thanks for helping to get this effort off the ground. Most notable among them is Sheilah Mann of APSA, who inspired, goaded, and subsidized it to completion. Thanks also to Cathy Hall, who typed and organized the materials, demonstrating a far better understanding of what I had in mind than I ever had. But the volume is really the product of all those political scientists who, for one reason or another, took the Simple Simulations short course. Many of them are represented herein, but more are not. I hope they learned something from me—I know I did from them.

Minneapolis
November, 1979

I. The Simple Simulation

A simple simulation, as the term is used here, is a "game" in the sense that participants are placed in roles which require that they overcome obstacles in pursuit of goals. To be "simple," in our sense, the game must be one which can be carried on without the use of computers or other more-or-less exotic equipment or facilities. Finally, it should not require administration or supervision beyond the capacities of an instructor and, perhaps, one assistant. In short, we will be discussing role-playing games which can be utilized relatively conveniently under normal college classroom conditions.

Under this very general definition, a wide variety of games can be subsumed. Part III provides examples which differ from one another considerably. These examples reflect different "levels of analysis," a property which will be discussed at some length in Part II. But simulations can differ from one another in many other ways as well, and it may be useful to look at some of these at this point.

Nature of the Task

Participants in a simulation seek to attain goals, in the face of obstacles. The goals may be stipulated by the game: participants in a legislative simulation, for instance, may be told that their basic goal is to maximize the likelihood of their reelection: all other activities in the game, such as drafting bills, holding hearings, debating, persuading, etc., should be undertaken with that in mind. Different actors may be given different goals: in the legislative example, the "legislators" will have different constituencies to which they must respond, and some will impose more constraints than others. Or, one could instruct some legislators to seek mainly reelection, while orienting others toward seeking positions of leadership, or promoting an ideological position. In any event, a simulation which stipulates such goals should also provide a reasonable way to measure performance, such as opinion polls suggesting what constituents want: the legislator could then be evaluated according to how closely he or she seemed to reflect constituent preferences.

Alternatively, simulation participants may be asked to decide for themselves what their goals will be, within reasonable limits. Some of the pros and cons of this will be examined in chapter four. For now, it will do to point out that some firm sense of goals should be developed at the outset of the game, and evaluation, if there is to be any, should be based upon fulfillment of those goals. It is also normally the case, for political simulations at least, that the "realism" of the game depends upon the "realism" of the goals. If we want students to learn about the dilemmas of choice faced by political actors, we will normally try to place them in situations whose opportunities, constraints, and incentives resemble those found in real politics.

Obstacles and Constraints

Given goals, what are the obstacles? They may, obviously, be embodied in the conflicting goals pursued by other actors. Goal conflicts may be represented as zero-sum (pure conflict, no mutually beneficial compromise possible) as in, for instance, a simulated election campaign. Or, they may be portrayed as mixed-motive (opportunities exist for compromise), as would often be the case in a legislative environment. The nature of the "problems" in the real world is the best guide to structuring a simulation.

Conflict with the environment is also possible. If students in a simulation are interacting not only with one another but also with a simulated environment, interesting problems can occur. Legislators who must deal with constituents (which can be simulated by a program, or set of rules) as well as other legislators, have environmental problems. Simulated executive budget-makers, as another example, might, in the simulation, have to deal in person only with one another. But the simulation model could also contain some rules governing the probable response of "Congress" to the budgetary product. If the student budget-makers are aware of this environment, and of at least roughly how it works, they must then treat it as an obstacle, one which does not allow them to solve their allocation problems, for instance, by giving more money to everybody.

A final obstacle, or constraint, worth noting is the rules of the game. Any simulation must have rules limiting the behavior of the participants. Parliamentary procedure in a legislature is one common example. Rules against using physical force, rules stating how many votes are needed to win, or rules stating how long a session may last are others. Students in a simulation must seek their objectives within a framework of such rules. Of course, a simulation may be designed so that the rules can be modified, either by the participants or by the simulation director. But even then, modifications are themselves usually governed by rules.

Resources

The participant in a simulation pursues individual or group goals, in the face of obstacles and constraints, by manipulating certain resources. The nature of these resources will vary with the content of the game. In a legislative game, position (e.g., party office, or committee chair) provides resources, as does substantive expertise. In an international politics game, the military and economic capability with which a simulated nation is endowed will constitute resources to be manipulated by the nation's leaders. Personal attributes, such as the ability to persuade or to assert one's self will be important resources in any game which provides opportunities for interpersonal interaction. Information, about other players, about issues, or about the rules of the game itself, will often be a manipulable resource.

Some of these resources, such as the particular abilities or characteristics of participants, will not be especially controllable by the game designer or instructor. In designing a game, however, one does make choices about whether or how to furnish or deny opportunities for these attributes to matter. Other resources, though, can be controlled (e.g., access to information about the game, or about the strategy and strength of others), or simply furnished (e.g., positions of formal leadership). The design of a game tends to dictate what kinds of resources will matter, and in what ways.

Number of Participants

The minimum is one. A game in which one student copes with a programmed environment is a useful teaching device, both because the range of things that can happen is fairly closely controlled (by whoever designs the simulation, i.e., creates the environment and the rules of the game) and because such exercises can be used with classes of virtually any size. They can even be assigned as homework.

Most simulations, however, involve interpersonal interaction. Indeed, this is often claimed among their virtues. Politics is in large part a matter of dealing with other people, while studying politics is typically a process of reading, writing, and listening. Simulation is one way to get beyond that. The number of people that can be accommodated in a simulation varies, of course, with the content of the simulation and the kind of interaction one wishes to see happening. If one is the minimum, the maximum cannot be stated so confidently. A simulated political convention could, in principle, contain as many participants as a real one. Whether anyone would have the facilities or the ambition to attempt that, however, is an open question. But it certainly is true that simulations can be large. The popular "Presidential Election" simulation by Weinbaum and Gold, for instance, can accommodate at least 152 participants at a time. Indeed, the minimum for this game is 45. More commonly, though, simulations tend to be designed for groups somewhere in the 15-50 range.

The number of participants in a game need not depend particularly upon the number of participants in the real world system being simulated. Real world phenomena (technically, "referents") can be reduced in scale (e.g., a "Senate" need not have 100 members, but could get by with 30) or reduced even more by what might be called abstraction. Thus, an international system may be represented by as few as 15 or so students, through both scaling down the system (to, say, five nations) and allowing each nation to be "played" by a three-person team.

Timing

A simulation may last anywhere from a few minutes to several hours, or more. A small, finite task need not take long, even if it is repeated. A legislature, on the other hand, can go on indefinitely. Simulations can be designed to be played as units, i.e., start to finish, without stopping, or to be broken into periods. The periods may represent natural breaks in the action, as when a legislative game is broken into periods of committee work, followed by periods of plenary session. Or, the periods may simply reflect convenience: games without natural breaks may be played until, for instance, the class is over for the day, then resumed when desired.

Physical Layout

The nature of the physical layout of a simulation depends, of course, upon the nature of the game itself and the number of people involved. The minimum requirement is simply a room large enough to accommodate the players who need to occupy it, plus tables and chairs. One can simulate many things—a city council, a summit conference, the Supreme Court—in a small room. A simulation of a political convention or a large legislative body would, even with some heroic scaling down, require more space.

Many simulations require more than one room. This is because they divide into subgroups. If a legislative simulation incorporates committees, for instance, it will probably be necessary to provide several rooms for them to meet in. Physical separation of players or teams is also useful when one wishes to restrict or prevent communication among them. In simulating an international crisis, for instance, one would not want the various "heads of state" all seated around a table, talking to one another freely. Separating them physically and imposing restrictions on the length and volume of messages which could be sent would probably enhance the realism of such an exercise.

In many simulations, it is also useful to create a "control" room, where those managing the game can work in some privacy. Since the game managers will typically be "playing" the environment in those games which have one (i.e., receiving data or decisions from the players, and transforming them, via game rules and formulas, into legitimate acts or environmental responses), privacy is required. To illustrate: in some international relations simulations, a sneak attack is possible. Usually this proceeds when the attacker files some sort of declaration of attack, specifying targets and weapons used, with the game managers. They may then have to compute, according to the rules, the immediate physical consequences of the attack—after first checking to make sure that the attacker in fact possesses all the resources designated for use. This checking, incidentally, requires that complete information on the state of the system (e.g., who has how much weapons) be on file with the game managers. Clearly, in a game of incomplete information (which international politics is, in general), such data and activities should not be accessible to just anybody. Hence the need for a control room, and for appropriate security.

Even in games where full information is available to all participants, or, if held in confidence, is held by the participants (e.g., a small legislative simulation in which all activity is conducted verbally, across the table), a control room can be useful. If a relatively inexpensive intercom system is available, it can be used to monitor the simulation without the physical presence of an instructor or other "authority." However, we are more concerned to point out that such equipment is not really necessary than to stress its advantages.

Control of the Game

Because simulations are run according to rules, they require the presence of someone to interpret and enforce those rules. Typically, this will be the instructor, whose main role will be that of umpire. But the instructor is apt to be involved in other aspects of the game, as well. The initial assignment of students to roles, the provision and explanation of game materials (manuals, forms to fill out, or whatever), and even such chores as transmitting messages, either to an individual or to the entire group, are often handled by the instructor.

Beyond such housekeeping, the instructor, or whoever manages the game, will usually play the role of "nature" in games where the players and the environment interact. This may be primarily a paperwork job: receiving written inputs, such as resource allocation decisions, and acting upon them in the name of the environment, according to the rules governing environmental response. Sometimes, though, a measure of discretion is involved in such chores. For instance, in "Politics and the Policy-Making Process" and "Congress Decides," legislators can poll their constituents to find out what is desired of them. The legislative districts, in these games, are based upon real ones, but there certainly is no reliable way to find out exactly how the inhabitants of any particular district would in fact react to the particular questions a student may have put to them. In this case the instructor, armed with all available data about the district, is asked to make his or her best guess and pass it along as an authoritative statement about the will of the people. At least, though, this is a between-sessions activity, and thus there is time for reflection. Other simulations may require that judgments must be made immediately so that the game can go on. However, this can be avoided in the design of a simulation, if desired.

An instructor who really wishes to get involved, or who simply wants to make things a bit more exciting, can play "nature" even more aggressively by randomly or strategically manipulating the environment. Most simulations in which there is an active environment can be made to accommodate this, if it is desired. Thus, in a stable but dull international system, one may interject a crisis (an assassination attempt, for instance, or nuclear proliferation) to which the players must improvise a response. There is a certain danger in this, though. An overenthusiastic manipulation of nature can so confound the development of carefully-laid plans and strategies that the players never get a sense of the outcomes of their best efforts. This can be frustrating, and can actually interfere with learning, if carried to extremes.

Conclusion

A simple simulation is an operating model of some aspect of political reality. As such it reflects a theoretical understanding of that reality, and presumably communicates that understanding. It may be all-man, or man-machine, provided in the latter case that the "machine" operation is rather simple. It places students in a realistic political environment, confronted by the following elements:

1. A role to play, in conjunction with others who also play roles.

2. A goal or set of goals to work toward.

3. Obstacles to goal-attainment, such as the conflicting goals of other players, or the resistance of the environment.

4. Constraints, in the form of game rules, limited information about the intentions of behavior of other players or the environment, or time.

5. Resources, such as interpersonal skills, information, or game-defined commodities (e.g., nuclear weapons).

The game then proceeds over a (roughly) predetermined period, culminating in some attainment of group and individual outcomes. Often, individual evaluation (but not necessarily grades) may be made on the basis of these outcomes. The simulation is usually followed by a discussion of what went on, and what can be learned from it.

II. The Objectives of Simulation

It is not uncommon for someone with some experience doing simulations to encounter, from a colleague, the question, "What is a good simulation for (whatever) course?" The best answer to that is, "It depends on what you're trying to do in there." In part, this answer is recommended because it conceals ignorance, at least for a time. However, it also shows wisdom, in that it recognizes that simulations differ substantially in their foci and, presumably, in their effects. Simulations can portray many aspects of political "reality," but no simulation presents the best possible model of all aspects of any given reality.

In this section, we will attempt to sort out some of the kinds of concepts and behaviors which can be represented by simulations, broken down and discussed in terms of their components. The discussion will be organized, for the most part, according to a levels-of-analysis scheme. This is not, we hasten to point out, the only way this organizing task could be approached. But, we think it is a useful approach to sorting out the goals and strategies of simulation design. Concrete illustrations of each of our types appear in Part III, and the reader may well find it useful to refer to them in connection with this and subsequent discussions.

The following scheme is more suggestive than precise. Its categories are not mutually exclusive, as simulations tend to be more complex and more flexible than our categories. We are not convinced, either, that these categories coincide particularly well with anybody's approach to the definition of teaching objectives—although, upon reflection, we have found them to be well enough related to our own approaches as to be useful. In any case, we will break our discussion of objectives down into the following categories:

1. Individual Decision-Making
2. Negotiation and Bargaining
3. Legislative Structure and Process
4. Systemic Models

Individual Decision-Making

Virtually any simulation can teach something about individual decision-making, as the making of decisions by individuals is the main thing going on in most games. The question here is simply one of emphasis. Two considerations are relevant to the discussion. First, a focus on individual decision-making suggests that what is to be learned is something about the kinds of decisions actually encountered by individuals in some real-world context. Thus, for this purpose, simulations which represent collective entities in the form of individual actors (e.g., an individual may play the "foreign office" or the "Supreme Court") are probably less valuable than those which offer a one-to-one relationship between referent system individuals and roles in the simulation. This is certainly true if one is attempting, among other things, to develop in students some empathy for real-world actors. The logical problems associated with the decisional role, however, may be essentially the same in both types of model. But the model which attempts to directly represent the behavior of referent individuals permits the subsequent discussion of the effects of individual-level variables (e.g., anxiety, inexperience, personality) in a manner which can be generalized plausibly to the real world. To discuss the behavior of collective entities in such terms requires the making of some questionable analogies—e.g., the State Department can be portrayed as "indecisive," but that may not mean quite the same thing at that level as the same term means when applied to an individual.

Second, whatever the nature of the model, an emphasis on individual decision-making requires the designer to pay conscious attention to the kinds of variables that students are expected to come to understand. At a minimum, this means that those variables which define the decisional situation must be designed with a teaching objective (either replication of some referent reality or operationalization of a theoretical model) in mind. A suggestive list of such variables would include: the presence or absence of a ready-made list of alternatives for consideration; the nature of available information regarding the outcomes of those alternatives; the availability of means for generating either additional alternatives or additional information; and the quantity and quality of available feedback once a choice has been made.

Decisions imply alternatives, but one can readily vary the amount of effort or expense required to generate them. A simulation scenario can simply provide them—as is often the case with very simple, one-person games, in which the individual simply chooses from among a set of possible decisions, on the basis of some information provided and, presumably, some rules or hypotheses which have been learned. Alternatively, one can provide the scenario or problem, complete with information (or, if you are so inclined, with instructions as to where relevant information might be found), with the burden of formulating plausible alternatives placed on the student. It will normally become obvious to students, in the latter condition, that searching for alternatives is costly. It requires effort, and it takes time. Since time constraints are likely to be built into any simulation, these costs will be clear, perhaps even to the point where reasonably thorough search will not always be carried out. Instructions can be provided to warn students of this pitfall, or they may be permitted to simply fall in.

The organizational costs of searching for alternatives can best be represented in simulations which are complex enough to involve interdependent behavior. There, time constraints can be enforced by the behavior of other simulators, given the need either to coordinate or to counter hostile acts immediately. Also, the costs of diverting people from whatever else they may have been doing to assist in a decision-making simulation which is designed to be playable by one individual can be made to accommodate the representation of some interpersonal or organizational variables, by having a team rather than a single person address the problem. The team may or may not be hierarchically structured, with explicit role-definition and division of labor. Indeed, one interesting exercise is to assign students a decisional task (an out-of-class assignment, if desired), then assign the same people to teams and have them deal with the same problem again. The well-known "risky-shift" phenomenon may be one outcome of this approach—or, depending on how you do it, it may not.

Information regarding the outcomes of alternative choices is comparatively easy to control or vary, and will have substantial effect upon the nature of the decision processes in the simulation. If relatively precise information is available, the decision problems become analytical exercises: known techniques can be employed to optimize the outcomes. If considerable uncertainty prevails, then the problem of choosing becomes more difficult, and the task of finding appropriate criteria by which to make (and perhaps defend) a choice becomes central. In any case, many possibilities exist for the simulation designer. Where alternatives are specified, one can state their consequences precisely—but one can still complicate the problem, by either expressing them in terms of more than one value (e.g., dollars spent, lives lost), or by presenting alternatives whose expected values are close, but which differ considerably in amount of risk involved (e.g., a modest gain with a high probability, as compared with a large gain, but with a lower probability).

Where a simulation faces the decision-maker with the requirement of searching for alternatives, it also imposes upon him/her the need to evaluate them. The designer, who presumably cannot anticipate all of the alternatives available in a complex problem (e.g., a simulated Secretary of State, ordered to make one and only one proposal to the government of Israel), can nevertheless provide useful information. In particular, the designer can help to guide the search and evaluation process by including precedents, actual or fictitious. A knowledge of what has gone before can be greatly helpful in making difficult decisions—or it can lead to a less-than-constructive incrementalism. Either way, precedent can be an interesting input to the decision problem.

Feedback is crucial to decision-making simulations, even though the intent of the simulation is not necessarily to train students to make particular kinds of decisions in the "best" way. Only through feedback, and perhaps some opportunity to repeat the exercise, can the student understand how a decision translates into consequences, and speculate on the possible consequences of choices not made. The most critical element in the provision of feedback, though, is not just the data, but an intelligible explanation of how the data were generated. In other words, the student must understand *why* particular choices led to particular outcomes, and why other choices would have turned out differently. This requires that the model of the "environment" which generated those outcomes be fully explained (and subjected to criticism, where appropriate). Or, where the feedback comes from human actors elsewhere in the simulation, there should be an attempt on the part of the instructor to reconstruct their response so, again, the decision-maker gets an idea of why things came out the way they did.

The variables associated with individual decision-making can be simulated in a number of ways. As noted, the simulations may be one-person exercises, or subroutines of more complex games. The "costs" of search may, in the absence of a social context, be simply those of looking up material in a game manual or in the library. Or, in the context of a larger game, such resources as staff persons or consultants may be brought into the picture. The main point, though, is that care must be taken to attend to the various properties of the decision situation so that these can be systematically taught, both as they occur in the game and as they occur in nature.

Negotiation and Bargaining

Like decision-making, bargaining is inherent in most political activity and in most political simulations as well. While the exercises discussed above involve either the activity of a single individual or, if collective, a cooperative relationship, they do not generally imply bargaining or conflict-resolving behavior. But most political simulations do, in some respects at least, involve such behavior. While the setting may be varied (international politics, collegial courts, legislative committees, or bureaucratic agencies), most simulation designers seem to view bargaining as central to the image of the referent system which they want a simulation to portray.

A clear definition of the goals sought by each party is necessary for effective bargaining. An individual need not know his/her opponent's goal structure, but must be fairly certain of his/her own. This can most easily be achieved by simply defining the situation for the bargainers, and in a model designed primarily to produce bargaining behavior, that is not a bad idea. However, when bargaining emerges out of the activities associated with a more complex simulation, it is most likely that the issues and positions at stake will have been defined by the participants. Thus the clarity with which these have been defined becomes one item for subsequent discussion and analysis. An additional virtue of requiring students to develop and state their bargaining positions themselves is that it provides a subtle way to introduce research on a substantive issue. Moreover, a greater attachment to positions can be expected from students who have formulated the positions themselves than from those who have simply had them dictated by a game manual.

Any bargaining situation, i.e., a mixed-motive problem in which there are elements of both conflict and potential cooperation, can serve to elicit interesting tactics. However simple the problem, for instance, bargainers must decide whether to pursue a "hard" line, conceding little or nothing but risking failure to agree at all, or a "soft" line, initiating concessions at the risk of being exploited. However, the basic problem can be made more interesting, both to play and to analyze, if the scenario provides an opportunity for one or both parties to inflict some sort of sanction for non-compliance (and thus to threaten to use it), and/or some kind of reward for cooperation (and thus to promise it). In simulations which are closely tied to a referent reality, the presence of such variables will be dictated by that referent system. Where learning about bargaining *per se* is a major objective, the presence of such factors can be varied.

Bargaining situations can be further complicated in several ways. One can, for instance, introduce an issue on which no agreement can possibly be attained as a kind of preliminary to the discussion of more tractable issues. The objective is to give participants a change (1) to experience the kind of frustration that even honest, reasonable people feel when they want to agree, but simply can't, and (2) to discover other issues on which agreement is possible, if they can avoid becoming fixated on the most attractive, but difficult, one. This illustrates an important element of the typical bargaining relationship, but one which is too often overlooked in discussions of the topic: creativity in finding a fruitful issue to negotiate.

Another complicating factor which can be introduced is the presence of more than two parties. While most formal theory pertaining to bargaining assumes two parties, the behavioral complications of having either neutrals, and hence mediators, present, or of having the potential for alliances built in, are interesting and worth exploring. Moreover, the theory of coalition-formation is itself an interesting aspect of the political behavior literature which can perhaps be taught better through simulation than any other way.

Two "practical" aspects of bargaining games deserve mention here. One is that such bargaining is unlikely to limit itself to the classroom unless the simulation is brief enough to be concluded in one session. Otherwise, participants will likely continue the interaction wherever they can. There is really nothing wrong with this, unless you are trying to do a little research on them at the same time you educate them. Indeed, it tends to bring the subject matter a little closer than average to the lives of the students. They should be advised, of course, not to feed any tips to others, who may be waiting their turn to try the same exercise.

Second, in simple bargaining situations, at least, you are likely to have some control over the length of time permitted to the negotiators. This can be creatively varied, so as to create crises, for instance. However, under some circumstances, at least, you may not want to tell the participants when the thing will end. This is simply because in bargaining games (and to some extent in all simulations), behavior can get a bit bizarre on what is known to be the final round.

Legislative Structure and Process

A "legislative" simulation, as the term is used here, is a representation of a collegial decision-making body. This definition is broad enough to encompass not only law-making bodies at any level of government, but also processes in other branches of government which strongly resemble the legislative. Thus, we would place in this category administrative simulations, insofar as the simulated bureaucrats are expected to engage in bargaining and policy decision-making in addition to, or instead of, such activities as managing others or keeping records. Judicial simulations, which nearly always represent the bargaining and voting activities of members of collegial courts, would also fall within this definition.

A legislative simulation, since it represents the behavior of individual "legislators" (or whatever), contains most of the characteristics discussed above in connection with individual decision-making and negotiation. But it also will tend to include variables of structure and process characteristic of collegial bodies, and will tend to place considerable emphasis upon them. The features of such a setting may include a committee system, or some equivalent means of dividing labor; formal, perhaps variable voting rules (e.g., a 2/3 vote required for some measures, majority for others); a party structure, or some other stable, visible basis of coalition; some sort of hierarchical leadership structure, with leaders possessing some kinds of formal sanctions as well as, perhaps, some informal leadership resources (e.g., information); and an issue agenda consisting of several, perhaps unrelated, matters, the attitudes and intensities of individuals differing with respect to these matters (thus permitting some logrolling). While the basic decisional and bargaining dimensions remain, specific outcomes will be significantly influenced by structural factors, and learning what these are and how they tend to affect outcomes becomes one of the simulation's main objectives.

With this category, we actually come closer to the thrust of most commercially available simulations than we have been thusfar. We have dwelt upon the other matters at length, though, because we consider them to be building blocks of decent "legislative" games. Indeed, we would recommend approaching the building of one of these by starting with the role requirements and behavioral options available to each potential participant rather than by looking at some overall model of structure. If this difference seems elusive, we stress it only because we have seen a number of simulations which seem to decently reflect the structure of some system or other, but which do not turn out to be very interesting or useful in practice because the individual roles are too often either barren of interesting possibilities, or badly distorted in order to fit the simple constraints of the model. It is students we are teaching, and they play individual roles, so start there.

In any case, though, the main purpose of the "legislative" simulation is to portray the system, and this can basically be achieved through a combination of the kinds of variables listed earlier in a manner decently reflective of the particular structure being modeled. Of course some systems have peculiar characteristics which are very difficult to simulate: how, for instance, can you reproduce the "power" of a veteran committee chairperson, or the norms of a judicial body. Suffice it for now to say that you can give it a try.

Systemic Models

The distinction between "legislative" and "systemic" is in one sense so subtle as to be artificial (legislative models are, of course, systemic or subsystemic), but the meaning here is fairly straightforward. Where the legislative models preserves an approximate one-to-one relationship between students and simulated individuals (e.g., Student X plays Senator Heartbleed, or at least a prototypical "liberal" role), in a systemic model the student plays the role of an institution. International politics simulations, where national decision-making systems are represented by anywhere from one to five actors, are a good example of this. Large organization processes are, in these models, reduced to individual or small group behavior. The plausibility of such models for scientific generalization may be questioned, but the teaching application does not really depend upon any belief that large organizations really behave like individual students. The objective is simply to provide for the students a sense of system structure and process.

Curiously, one implication of the difference between systemic and legislative simulations is that the former require less care in realistic role definition. The plausible fear of distorting for students the role of, say, a Congress member, is less threatening when one realizes that the simulation, however good it may be, is taking the heroic leap of having one sophomore act as the Russian military establishment. In other words, the focus upon individual and interpersonal behavior which we value so highly in the other models discussed here is simply less valuable in this case. Such simulations, then, can be designed with institutional relationships primarily in mind, and with the intent of portraying such gross relationships and introducing the kinds of resources which are employed by the institutions in question, the kinds of policy options which they may face, and the sorts of difficulties they have with one another.

The fact that institutional behavior is not all that much like interpersonal behavior should, of course, be noted in discussing the simulation. One additional precaution which can be taken to prevent interpersonal attitudes and skill from overwhelming the structural relationships you are trying to focus upon is to make sure that the simulation is conducted on a relatively impersonal basis. You can, for instance, forbid face-to-face communication for the most part, relying instead upon written notes. Physical separation of the players can also work to this end—indeed, they need not even play at the same time or in the same place, as long as communication via note or some equivalent is sufficient to carry the game along.

Conclusion

The message of this chapter is simply that each designer or user of simulation should give some thought to exactly what is supposed to be learned from a simulation before designing or choosing one for the classroom. Our breakdown of simulations by level of analysis, more or less, is intended mainly to be suggestive of the kinds of questions one might ask prior to deciding upon a particular approach to simulation. At the very least, we hope that the foregoing typology is convincing on the point that there is no simulation that can plausibly claim to teach "everything" about a particular referent system, or to be in every way the "best" simulation of it. What is best, to repeat our earlier suggestion, depends entirely upon what you are trying to achieve.

III. The Simulations

Politics and the Policy-Making Process

Anne Walcott
Gustavus Adolphus College

Ann Wynia
North Hennepin Community College

SUBJECT MATTER: The policy-making process.

APPROPRIATE COURSE AND LEVEL: Introductory American Government (could be adapted for State Government).

DESCRIPTION OF CONTEXT: This simulation of the legislative policy process includes the Legislature, the Executive Branch and Interest Groups.

The Legislature. The Legislature is composed of ___*___ members, ___*___ of whom are Democrats, ___*___ of whom are Republicans. Each party is led by a Party Leader. The Democratic leader is referred to as the Majority Leader while the Republican leader is referred to as the Minority Leader. At the beginning of the first session each party will caucus to choose the following. Each party determines its own method of choosing.

Democrats	Republicans
1. Majority Leader (Speaker)	1. Minority Leader
2. Chairpersons of the Legislative Committees	2. Ranking Minority Member of Legislative Committees (optional)
3. Party Whip (optional)	3. Party Whip (optional)

All legislators are members of either the Human Resources Committee or the Commerce Committee. Each of these committees is chaired by a Democrat. The function of the committees is to give preliminary consideration to all bills brought before the legislature. They may conduct investigations and hear testimony from any witnesses they choose to invite. The Committee must vote upon a bill before it can be brought to the full legislature for passage. If a committee votes favorably on a bill, it automatically goes onto the docket for

---

*Numbers depend on the size of the class.

14

consideration by the Legislature. A negative committee vote on a bill prevents the bill from coming to the full legislature.

The Executive Branch. The Executive Branch consists entirely of Republicans. Its component offices are ___*___ legislative liaisons who speak for the President and are responsible for the passage of his/her legislative program. The legislative liaisons will present the President's legislative proposals to the Assembly, but should find friendly legislators who will serve as the official sponsor of any bill. The success of the executive branch will be largely judged by the fate of these legislative proposals.

Interest Groups. There are two interest groups. Their function is to attempt to influence legislators and the executive to propose and to pass legislation desired by the membership of their group, and to oppose legislation felt to be harmful to the interests of their membership.

The interest groups are:

1. The Americans for Constitutional Action (ACA). This is an ideologically conservative group. It will be free to determine its goals and particular interests, but must operate within the framework of conservative political beliefs. In real life ACA describes itself as favoring individual rights, sound money, fiscal integrity, and private market, local self-government, and strengthening of national sovereignty, while being against group morality, a socialized economy, inflation, price controls, central-government intervention in local affairs, coercion of individuals through government regulation, and any surrender of control of foreign or domestic affairs to any other nation or to any international organization.

2. The Americans for Democratic Action (ADA). This is the liberal counterpart of the ACA and functions in the same manner from its liberal point of view. ADA members have generally pushed for New Deal type legislation and against rising defense spending and encroachments on civil liberties.

NUMBER OF PLAYERS: 20-25 players should be the minimum number of players. There is no maximum.

NUMBER OF ROLES:

1. *Majority Leader.* The Majority Leader is also automatically the Speaker of the House and as such, presides over all full sessions of the Legislature. If the Majority Leader is unable or does not care to preside at any time, he/she may appoint a substitute. The Majority Leader may vote on all bills. The Majority Leader is also in charge of scheduling bills for a vote by the full assembly and determines when and if a bill is voted on. Finally the Majority Leader is also his/her party's leader and as such may call for meetings of the Democratic Caucus.

2. *Minority Leader.* The Minority Leader is head of the Republican Party and as such is responsible for passing minority legislation and opposing majority

party legislation.

3. *Whips.* If elected by either party, the whips are responsible for getting support for their party's legislation and opposing legislation of the opposing party.

4. *Chairpersons of the Legislative Committees.* The Chair of each committee has the power to decide which bills will be considered and to limit the time of consideration if he/she desires. He/she must also invite all witnesses (legislators not members of the committee, representatives of the president, and interest groups) to testify on bills. The Chair presides at committee meetings.

5. *Interest Group Lobbyists.* There should be at least two members per interest group. Interest group lobbyists may use any reasonable means in pursuing their goals. The interest group member has two main tasks. He/she must get those positions his/her group prefers adopted by the legislature and by the president and must block those measures the group opposes. He/she will be evaluated according to how effective he/she is in reaching these goals. Components of the evaluation by all other members of the political system and the supervisor will include ratings of his/her expertise, diligence, persuasiveness, and capacity for bargaining.

Each interest group must submit at least two pieces of legislation, but must find a friendly Congressperson to officially sponsor the legislation. Throughout the simulation the interest groups should communicate via the blackboard or other means their stands on bills being considered by the legislature. At the close of the simulation each interest group will select a group of bills in which they have been especially interested and rate each legislator according to what percent of the time he/she voted in the way favored by the interest group. Interest group members also have a certain amount of money to contribute to campaigns.

6. *Executive Branch Members* (Presidential Liaisons). There should be at least two liaisons, more depending on class size. They will be evaluated by the degree to which they can get the President's program accepted by the Legislature and prevent the passage of objectional legislation, and by a rating by other members of the political system and the supervisor of their bargaining skill, expertise, persuasiveness, etc.

Presidential liaisons should work together in preparing the president's proposals and lobbying them through the legislature. The president's proposals should number at least three. The President may take stands on bills sponsored by others and communicate these to members of the legislature.

In order to influence legislators to cooperate, the executive branch will have three main weapons. First, the President's position will have a significant impact upon public opinion nationwide. Second, he controls certain monetary and patronage resources. He controls some campaign funds (relevant only to Republican legislators) which he may give or withhold as he sees fit. Also he has a certain number of government job favors which he may give to the constituents of any legislator (either party) who pleases him, thus increasing the legislator's popularity in this district. Finally the President may veto bills if the legislature is still in session. Vetoes may be overridden by a 2/3 vote.

7. *Legislators.* Probably the minimum number of legislators (which could

include the two committee chairs, whips, Minority Leader) would be 13.

A legislator's main task is to get reelected. To do this he/she must keep his/her constituents at least reasonably satisfied with his/her performance. How closely he/she must attend to this will be determined by how strong the opposition party is in his/her district. This "security factor" is indicated on the role definition sheet (Appendix A). Districts are a sample of real congressional constituencies.

To find out how the folks back home are reacting to what he/she does, the legislator has two devices she/he can rely on:

a. Interest group reactions. She/he must interpret this in terms of his/her judgment of how influential each group probably is in his/her district. He/she may infer this from the profile of his/her constituency which is provided as well as from the information about how the real life Congressperson votes (which presumably tells us something about constituency views) (see Appendix A). Strong interest group support or opposition may be important to reelection chances so the legislator should pay attention to these groups. At the end of the simulation the groups will have to allocate their funds to support or oppose legislators whom they like or dislike.

Also, each interest group will at the end of the simulation rate all legislators and this rating will be used to determine constituency satisfaction.

b. Public opinion polls. Each session each legislator may formulate two questions to be asked of her/his constituents by the Reliable Poll and reported at the beginning of the next session. Responses are guaranteed accurate, but their quality depends upon the quality of the questions asked. Questions must be submitted in duplicate to the instructor or no answer will be returned.

In addition, the President has certain resources which he may distribute to help or hinder the re-election chances of legislators.

A second major indicator of the success of a legislator is her/his internal prestige. This will be determined at the close of the simulation by polling the other members of the political system, asking them to rate all other participants. Some of the components of the internal prestige rating will be reliability, leadership, diligence, persuasiveness, etc. The instructor in his/her role of Game Supervisor will also contribute to this rating. The score on the quiz which will cover the explanation and rules of this game will be used to determine the legislator's expertise rating.

Defying one's constituency and pursuing one's conscience can be rewarded in this rating, but it will cost you with the voters.

OPTIONAL ROLES: Roles can be added by simply expanding the number of legislators, interest group members or executive branch members.

LENGTH OF TIME REQUIRED: The minimum amount of time required would be about seven 50-minute class periods. This simulation has been run for an entire semester, one day a week, quite successfully. When this is done, more preparation can be required in terms of written legislation and position papers on their legislation.

HOW MANY DISTINCT PERIODS: Below is a sample schedule for the simulation.

Session No.	Class Time	Activity
		Role selection. This is essentially done by the instructor. A sheet can be passed around asking which roles and party the students wish to assume for the simulation.
		Roles given out. Lobbyists and Liaisons may be asked to meet with the instructor outside of class for further instructions as to their roles.
1	50 min.	Legislation due. Test on rules of simulation (see Appendices B and C for rules and sample test). If desired, the students can be required to give a brief statement to the class describing their constituency.
2	50 min.	Party caucuses choose legislative leaders. Presidential liaisons and lobbyists may attend caucuses of their choice but not vote. Liaisons and lobbyists should find legislators who will sponsor their bills.
		Students should fill out their Personal Reaction Form which is due the next session (this is optional, see Appendix E for sample form).
3	50 min.	Personal Reaction Form due (optional). Committee hearings.
4	50 min.	Committee hearings. Begin voting on legislation.
5	50 min.	Committee hearings. Finish voting on legislation.
6	50 min.	Assembly vote on legislation.
7	50 min.	Figure scores for simulation (see Appendix D for score sheet).
		Evaluation papers due (see Appendix E for format).
		Simulation debriefing.
8	50 min.	Simulation debriefing.

Depending on how swiftly things proceed, a session may be dropped or added anywhere from sessions 3-6.

PHYSICAL AND/OR COMPUTATIONAL FACILITIES REQUIRED: A large room with at least two large tables and chairs for the two main committees should be available. Two separate rooms would also be desirable. Partitions in the case of the one room being used would be ideal. It is extremely advantageous to have a ditto machine close to the simulation room(s), since the students are required to write their legislation on dittos for the instructor to duplicate. As the simulation progresses, students may write or re-write legislation during the sessions, thus requiring their efforts to be duplicated immediately. Blackboards are also necessary for communication, especially by lobbyists.

HOW MUCH AND HOW LONG MUST PARTICIPANTS PREPARE: This is variable. The minimum preparation by all should be the creation of a piece of legislation (Appendix F includes the format for legislation). They must also have at least a day to study their constituency profile. Appropriate chapters in an American Government text on Congress, the Presidency, Interest Groups and Policy chapters on Domestic and Foreign Policy may also be required reading and tested before the simulation.

More elaborate preparation could include a position paper which would consist of the background of the legislation they want to present and the strategy they see necessary for its implementation. Additional substantive policy articles, books could be required reading.

EVALUATION: Quality of participation is not recommended as a component of the evaluation. Points are usually given for the submission of legislation, attendance, the simulation evaluation paper (see Appendix E) and the simulation quiz. These points are set and not allocated on the basis of quality.

APPENDIX A
Constituency Profile

Included with this profile is the following information:

1. Congressperson _____ *(Student's name, District)*

2. Committee Assignment

3. Party

4. Security Factor—this is a number from −3 to +3 which indicates how close the last election was. For example, a +3 tells the student that he/she won the last election by over 55%.

5. Additional constituency information may be found in *The Almanac of American Politics.*

APPENDIX B
Rules

1. In determining the results of any vote the number of members present and voting shall be used to determine the necessary percentage.

2. The initial assignment of bills to committee shall be determined by the instructor. The legislature may alter that assignment by a majority vote.

Committees

3. Committee chairmen have full voting rights in committees. Committee chairmen shall inform the Majority Leader when any bill has passed his/her committee so that the Majority Leader may arrange the voting schedule.

4. The Speaker/Majority Leader is not a voting member of either committee, but may attend and speak at committee sessions.

5. The Minority Leader is a voting member of his committee.

6. Committees have the power to amend bills referred to them. In the event of extensive revision a new written copy of the bill should be prepared for distribution.

Legislative Assembly

7. Debate on a given motion shall not exceed five minutes. No person shall speak more than two minutes if there is another person desiring to speak.

8. No bill may be amended on the floor more than twice. The subject matter of amendments is unrestricted.

9. All votes shall be by roll call. A person may abstain from voting.

10. Decisions of the Chairpersons and the Majority Leader may be overridden by a 2/3 vote of the appropriate body.

APPENDIX C
Simulation Rules and Procedures Quiz

Answer on this sheet.

_____ 1. In the legislative assembly, debate on a given motion shall not exceed:

   a. 5 minutes   b. 10 minutes   c. 15 minutes   d. 20 minutes

_____ 2. The Republican party is the majority in the legislative body. True/False

_____ 3. The Americans for Constitutional Action (in real life):

   a. favor maintaining a strong military defense
   b. favor lowering the debt ceiling
   c. oppose busing
   d. all of these

_____ 4. The Americans for Democratic Action (in real life):

    a. favor easier voter registration procedures
    b. oppose busing
    c. supported the war in Vietnam and advocated strong, decisive military action to win the war
    d. all of these

_____ 5. Which of the following statements about the simulated legislative process is NOT true?

    a. the President does not possess any veto power over legislation
    b. to be considered by the Assembly, a bill must first receive a favorable vote in committee
    c. the Majority Leader is responsible for scheduling bills for debate and voting in the General Assembly
    d. the committee chairpersons have the power to limit the amount of time spent on a bill in their committees

_____ 6. Twenty-four members are present and voting. To override a decision of the Majority Leader requires:

    a. 12 votes   b. 13 votes   c. 16 votes   d. 18 votes

_____ 7. Your grade in the course for the simulation exercise will be determined by whether you win or lose the game as defined by your particular role. True/False

_____ 8. Whether or not a legislator gets re-elected in this simulation will be determined simply by whether or not (s)he gets at least one piece of legislation passed. True/False

_____ 9. Once a bill has been passed out of committee it may not be amended by the General Assembly. True/False

_____ 10. Lobbyists and Presidential Liaisons:

    a. are not permitted to speak at committee hearings
    b. will not be able to influence whether or not a legislator gets re-elected in the simulation
    c. are not permitted to vote on legislation before the General Assembly
    d. all of these

You have until 15 minutes after the hour to complete the quiz. If you finish early, return this sheet to the instructor.

APPENDIX D
Legislative Score Sheet

The legislative score sheet may be handed out with the role selections or at the end of the simulation. It is advised that it be handed out with the role selections to emphasize the rewards and punishments inherent in the game. Part I is used for Lobbyists and Liaisons as well as Legislators. Parts II and III are only for Legislators. The Personal Convictions Score may be omitted if you don't use this aspect of the game.

Interest groups may contribute money to a Congressperson's opposition in the coming election. This is noted in Part II, *Campaign Contributions.* Note also that the contributions and patronage are recorded in terms of "units." Thus one monetary contribution unit could equal $10,000, while one patronage unit could equal ten jobs. This determination is left up to the instructor.

The peer group rating, a component of the Internal Power Score, Part I, is arrived at by asking the participants to nominate one individual simulation participant for each of the following categories:

1. Most Persuasive
2. Most Knowledgeable
3. Most Powerful

The Instructor's expertise rating in Part I is arrived at by using the score of each participant's test on the simulation given at the beginning of the game.

Legislative Score Sheet

_____
(Name, State, and District No.)

I. Internal Power Score

Score one point if you sponsored any legislation _____

How many bills authored by you received favorable committee action? _____ x 2 _____

How many bills authored by you were passed by the Assembly? _____ x 3 _____

Score one point for each of your bills signed by the President _____

Peer Group Rating _____

Instructor's Expertise Rating _____

TOTAL INTERNAL SCORE [____]

II. External Constituency Score

A. Real Life Group Ratings (taken from Constituency Profile):

ADA _____

ACA _____

At "a" write in the initials of the group giving the highest rating   a. _____
to the district's real life Congressman. If the two ratings are
within 40 points of each other write in both.

B. Simulation Group Ratings:

    ADA _____

    ACA _____

If there are 30 points difference or more between the two   b. _____
simulation ratings, at "b" write in the initials of the group
giving you the highest rating. If there is less than 30 points
difference write in the initials of both.

VOTING SCORE: If "a" and "b" are *exactly* the same, score +5.
                 If "a" and "b" are *exactly* the opposite, score −5.
                 If "a" and "b" are partially the same, score 0.   _____

Polling: Did you poll your constituents? _____
If yes, score 1; if no, score 0.   _____

If you polled your constituents about any bills that you later voted on in
the assembly, how many times did you vote the *same* as the most popular
opinion in your district (ignoring "no opinion" responses)?   x. _____

How many times did you vote *contrary* to the most popular opinion?   y. _____

Subtract "y" from "x."   _____

Campaign Contributions: List all campaign and patronage contributions

To you _____

To your opponent _____

Score 3 points for each contribution unit or patronage appointment
you received.   + _____

Subtract 3 points for every contribution to your opponent.   − _____

Security Factor (as assigned)   _____

                        TOTAL EXTERNAL SCORE

III. Personal Convictions Score

Out of _____ roll call votes in which I participated, I voted consistently
with my own personal convictions as listed on the personal reaction
record how many times?

              PERSONAL CONVICTIONS SCORE

IV. TOTAL LEGISLATIVE SCORE

Add internal, external, and personal convictions scores.

APPENDIX E
Simulation Evaluation Paper

1. Which aspects of the simulation were realistic (example rules, procedures,
events, legislation, roles)? Which aspects did not seem realistic? Why? (Use
your text for this as well as your own impressions.)

2. Discuss the various roles that were played in the simulation. Evaluate the performance of your colleagues in these roles.

3. Which groups were more effective? Explain.

   a. Democrats
   b. Republicans
   c. ADA
   d. ACA
   e. Presidential Liaisons

4. What personality traits do you feel made people more or less successful?

5. Evaluate your own role in the simulation.

6. Assess the value of the simulation as a whole to this course. (You may submit this last part separately without your name attached.)

APPENDIX F
Format for All Legislative Proposals

Title of Legislation

Sponsor(s): (Only a legislator's name appears here—use your own name.)

Author: (if someone other than the legislator such as President or Interest Group)

Substance of the Proposal:

All legislation must be on ditto paper.

Note: Depending on the time available for preparation, the substance of the proposed legislation can be more or less elaborate. If there is adequate time students can be given examples of real life legislation to study.

Congress Decides

Robert E. Eagle
University of Montana

1. *Subject Matter:* U.S. Congress.

2. *Courses and Levels for Which Simulation is Appropriate:* This simulation has been used both in introductory American Government classes and in upper level

Legislative Process classes. It has a moderate and somewhat flexible level of sophistication.

3. *Number of Participants:*

Minimum:	7
Maximum:	72
Optimum:	30

All participants play the role of legislator. Each player has a designated district, party affiliation, ideological orientation, and committee membership.

4. *Length of Time:*

Minimum:	3 hours
Maximum:	10 hours
Optimum:	8 hours

5. *Schedule of Activities:* The first part of the simulation consists of legislative committee meetings. These can take one or two hours. The second part of the simulation is floor debate. This can take from two to six hours. The debriefing takes about one hour.

6. *Required Physical Facilities:* The minimum requirement for the committee meetings is one large room with moveable chairs. All committees can meet in one room if necessary. It is helpful, but not necessary, to have separate rooms for the committees. For the floor debate a large room is necessary. Moveable chairs are not necessary for the floor debate; an auditorium type of seating can be used.

It is helpful if the person presiding over the floor debates has a gavel. This adds color to the proceedings, but it is not necessary.

7. *Preparation:* It is helpful, but not necessary, to have students do some research on the issues which will be considered by their own committees. It is also very helpful if the students have been given some basic information about the U.S. Congress, the committee system, and parliamentary procedure. Students can also do some research on Congressional voting records.

8. *Special Materials:* All students are given a copy of the 20 legislative proposals to be considered by the legislative assembly. Each committee is given some background information, consisting of pro and con arguments, for each bill which has been referred to that committee. Name tags are needed for the committee sessions and can also be used during the floor debates. It is helpful if a printed digest of the major elements of parliamentary procedure is given to each student.

9. *Other Features:* The legislative proposals are quite short and simple, and the background information is brief. This makes it possible to update the proposals

regularly to include issues currently before Congress. It is possible to have the students draft the bills themselves and develop the background information if there is sufficient course time available.

10. *Evaluation:* The *Congress Decides* simulation was run in an upper level Legislative Process class of seven students and in a lower level American Government course of 130 students, divided into two groups of 65. A structured rating form (copy attached as Appendix E) was used to facilitate student evaluations of the simulation in these classes. The ratings are shown in Table 1 below. For comparison, ratings from another simulation used in upper level State Government classes are provided. I consider *The New Alexandria Simulation* one of the best available.

TABLE 1
Student Evaluations of the Simulation
(Means on scale from a low of 1 to a high of 10)

Item Being Rated	Congress Decides Simulation (Lower Level) (N=102)	Congress Decides Simulation (Upper Level) (N=7)	The New Alexandria Simulation (N=18)
Objectives of the exercise clarified by instructor	7.13	7.71	7.11
Relation of simulation model to reality	5.89	8.14	6.22
Value of exercise as a learning device	7.36	8.29	7.67
Personal enjoyment of exercise	7.65	9.57	8.17
Amount of time spent in relation to the value of the exercise	7.43	8.29	7.06
Amount of time spent in relation to stated objectives for the exercise*	5.25	5.29	5.22

*The optimal rating on this item would be 5.50. On the other items the optimal rating would be 10.00.

The student ratings of the *Congress Decides* simulation in the Legislative Process class are the highest ratings I have ever had in over two dozen simulations I have run during the last 11 years. Students enjoyed the mix of issues, a point to keep in mind in deciding whether to present issues or have students choose the issues. Students would have liked more time to do substantive research on the issues. Some would have liked to draft the bills themselves. They would also have liked some input from *interest groups.* Such input could be incorporated in the background information issues given to the students, and it could be used in calculating reelection probabilities for participants.

In the American Government class, because of the large size of the groups used, individual poll information from constituents and election feedback were not provided. The ratings are lower than for the upper level class, but these ratings are comparable with ratings of other simulations I have used in lower division courses. Overall the students liked the simulation, although they made suggestions for improvement such as more time for substantive research.

11. *Narrative:* In the *Congress Decides* simulation, students play the roles of members of the U.S. Congress. Only one house of the Congress is set up, and this house bears more resemblance to the Senate than to the House of Representatives. There are 12 legislative districts, designated with geographical names such as Pacific Northwest or Deep South. Each participant is also given a party affiliation and an ideological orientation—conservative, moderate, or liberal. Party affiliations are assigned so that the Democrats have a seven to five majority in the legislature. Ideological orientations are assigned so that there are equal numbers of conservatives and liberals, with a small number of moderates who hold the balance of power ideologically.

If there are 12 or fewer participants, then there is only one legislator from each district. If fewer than 12 are taking part, district assignments should be made to preserve a balance between parties, between ideological orientations, and between sections of the United States.

If there are more than 12 participants, there will be more than one legislator from some or all districts. In this situation too, care should be taken to maintain a balance among parties, ideologies, and geographical areas.

It is not absolutely necessary that the students do individual research on their roles, particularly at the lower undergraduate level. Such research can be done if time permits, and it undoubtedly improves the quality of the simulation experience. There are two types of research which students can do which are useful preparation for the simulation. One is to look up the voting records of one or more legislators in the U.S. Congress on topics that will be covered in the simulation. One method I have used for such research is to designate a state within the geographical district used in the simulation. For example, Texas could be used to represent the Prairie South simulation district. The student or students who represent this district can go to a source such as the *Congressional Quarterly Almanac* and look up the votes of both senators from the states being used as their models, going back three or four sessions and looking specifically for votes on subject areas that will be discussed in the simulation. If both senators from a state have voted together most of the time, this fact should be noted. If, on the other hand, there is a wide divergence between the votes of the two senators, then the representatives from this district might conclude that they have considerable flexibility as to how they should vote in the simulation assembly.

The second type of research which students can do to prepare for the *Congress Decides* simulation is substantive research on the issues that will be considered and debated in the simulation. This may take a significant amount of time, and the instructor will have to decide how important a detailed substantive knowledge is to the simulation and whether this substantive research will fit into the course as a whole.

If the simulation is being run in an introductory American Government course with a total of three hours being devoted to the exercise, then it is probably not worth having the students do individual research of either of the two types mentioned. If the focus of the course is on substantive issues of American politics, then it may be very appropriate to have the students do some detailed research on substantive issues. If the course deals with the legislative process at the upper undergraduate or graduate level, then it may be useful to have the students engage in both of the types of individual research indicated.

In the *Congress Decides* simulation there are 20 legislative proposals which have been presented to the simulation assembly—19 bills and one resolution. These legislative proposals are quite short—generally from one to three sentences. All participants receive a copy of all 20 proposals.

There is also some background information, consisting of pro and con arguments, for each of the legislative proposals. This background information is brief, from one to three paragraphs. The background information is given only to members of the legislative committee to which the bills have been referred. This is intended to give the committee members greater knowledge of the issues before their committee so that during floor debate other members of the assembly will have to look to committee members for some guidance on bills reported out by that committee.

The legislative issues were chosen so that the lines of cleavage among legislators would be different for different issues. For example, some issues pose the question of federal government involvement versus leaving things in private hands, so that liberals will be opposing conservatives. Other issues are geographical in nature; a proposal to import water from the Columbia River to the Colorado River is one such issue. Thus the student participants soon discover that a person who is their opponent on one issue may be their ally on another.

The beginning of the simulation activity is a set of legislative committee meetings. Students can be assigned to committees on the basis of their preference. This is the best way to assign them in an upper level class where the number of students is not too large and where they have enough general knowledge of the subject areas to have a preference as to which committee they will be assigned to. An alternative method for assigning students in a large lower level course is by the alphabetical order of their names.

Six standing legislative committees are used in the *Congress Decides* simulation. The committees are: Agriculture, Armed Services, Energy and Natural Resources, Environment and Public Works, Foreign Relations, and Human Resources. In the simulation each committee has three or four bills assigned to it.

Committees should meet in a room or rooms with moveable chairs. For each committee chairs should be arranged in a circle. First each committee chooses a chairman, a vice chairman, and a secretary. If the committees have more than five persons each, these officers should all be of the majority party. However, if the committees are smaller than five the officers other than the committee chairman can be chosen without regard to party affiliation. In this situation students should be reminded that in the real Congress the committee leadership is always of the majority party, except that there is a designated ranking minority member.

After the committees have chosen their leaders, the chairman should take charge of the committee. Before formal discussion begins in the committee, some time should be allotted for informal discussion among participants. During this period students may wish to meet in party and/or ideological caucuses within the committee. Or individual legislators may wish to talk privately with others to discuss possible vote trades.

After the informal interaction period—generally five to ten minutes is sufficient—the committee convenes formal discussion on the legislative proposals which have been referred to the committee. They are told that for each bill they can adopt a do-pass recommendation, a do-not-pass recommendation, or one or more amendments to the bill. The secretary keeps a written record of committee actions, including the exact wording of any amendments, and gives this record to the instructor at the end of the committee deliberations.

After the committee sessions have been conducted, the entire legislative assembly meets for floor debate on some or all of the proposals which have been reported out favorably by the committees. Before the first session of floor debate, the instructor chooses three of the bills given top priority by three of the committees as "the President's Program." These three issues are scheduled first for floor debate. After this the top priority bills from other committees are scheduled, perhaps in alphabetical order of the committee names. One bill from each committee should be considered before a second bill from any committee is brought up. Time may permit no more than six bills to be considered; this will be the case if only three hours are devoted to the entire exercise, including two for floor debate.

If there is sufficient time, students should meet in ideological and party caucuses before the floor debate begins. First they meet in ideological caucuses—conservatives in one group, liberals in another group, and moderates in another. Fifteen minutes is sufficient for this caucus. In the caucus they discuss which issues they will support and which ones they will oppose. Then they meet for another 15 minutes in party caucuses, trying to decide which issues to work for or against as a party. It doesn't take long in the party caucuses for the Democrats to realize that there are some real splits within their party, and the same is true for the Republicans. Party leaders can be appointed by the instructor or chosen by the party members in the caucus. Someone should likewise be chosen to preside over each ideological caucus. Party leaders should be moderates in terms of ideology, and the moderate caucus is a place where the two party leaders can meet to discuss strategies and priorities. Incidentally, this arrangement keeps the party leaders out of the conservative and liberal caucuses so that alternate leadership is developed there.

After the party caucus there should be a period of free interaction in which members are free to move around the room and talk with any other representatives. This is a time when head counts may be taken to see where support and opposition lie on the legislative proposals which have been reported out by the committees. After this period of free action the floor debate is started.

If the simulation group is large, it is helpful to have the participants agree to a time limit for debate on each legislative proposal. A period of 10 to 15 minutes is usually sufficient. Debate is carried out following *Robert's Rules of Order*. In my simulations I have presided over floor debate myself. It would be possible, however, to have a student from the class do the presiding or to have a graduate assistant preside. If a student is presiding, the instructor can serve as parliamentarian.

It is helpful to record the votes on each bill or resolution so they can be mentioned in the discussion session which follows the floor debates. If the group is fairly small, the votes of each member on each issue can be recorded. These votes can then be used to give each participant some feedback on how likely it is that they will be reelected. If the group is large, it may not be feasible to keep a record on how each member votes. In this event it is not possible to give each member constituent feedback based on his/her voting record. This is one reason for keeping the simulation groups relatively small. A large class can be divided into smaller groups for the simulation to keep the group size manageable, provided there are graduate assistants or colleagues available to handle some of the groups. Another possibility is to schedule some groups at a time other than the regular class period.

During the simulation the participants may receive some limited information on how their constituents feel about the legislative proposals before the assembly. I have used a technique which has been described by Charles and Anne Walcott in their monograph, *Simple Simulations*. The technique is to provide for the simulation participants the results of opinion surveys taken by the Practically Omniscient Opinion Poll, or POOP. The students may receive survey results on only two questions per day of the simulation. At the end of each period they each submit up to two questions that they would like to have asked of their constituents. The poll results are handed out on a private, confidential basis at the beginning of the next period. The instructor derives poll figures from his/her own estimates of how constituents in various parts of the country would feel about the legislative issues being considered. Actual national and regional polls may be used as a guide in determining poll results. Such polls are frequently presented in the news media. Also, the instructor will have to use some seat-of-the-pants guesswork in arriving at poll results for each issue. The rick is to present these results to the students as though they have a very solid, s ientific foundation.

In the course of developing this simulation model, I wrote down some specific learning objectives for the exercise. This list of things which might be learned in the simulation is quite handy as a guide for the discussion or debriefing which follows the last session of floor debate. These learning objectives were also helpful to me in designing the simulation itself. The objectives are included below as Appendix A.

APPENDIX A
Congress Decides Simulation: Learning Objectives

These are things students should learn by participating in this simulation:

1. There are a large number of issues before a legislature at any given time. There needs to be some division of labor and specialization in order to facilitate in-depth study of these issues. Legislative committees are set up to provide this division of labor and specialization.

2. There are usually several bills pending before a legislative committee. The committee needs to set some priorities so they will know what to take up first.

3. A legislative committee has several options in dealing with a bill. They can simply let it sit. Or they can approve it as it is. Or they can amend it to meet suggestions of committee members and others who present information and recommendations to the committee.

4. There are generally bills which have been reported out of committees and are on the calendar(s) waiting for floor consideration. There needs to be some way for the bills to be scheduled according to an order of priority. Also, some determination needs to be made as to how much time of floor consideration will be allotted to each bill. Provision needs to be made for consideration of amendments as well as of the bill as reported out of committee.

5. The members of a committee generally know more about a bill than the other members of the legislature. Other members tend to look to committee members for guidance in deciding what should be done with a bill. However, the other members are not shy. Many of them will enter into the debate, especially if the issue is a major one, and also especially if the bill is on a subject that directly affects their constituency or about which a member happens to know a great deal even though he is not on the committee.

6. There are usually differences among committee members over what should be done with a bill. Committee members have to decide whether to bring these differences up on the floor or whether to stick together and present a united front during floor consideration, thereby enhancing the chances of getting the bill approved as it was reported by the committee.

7. There are formal rules of parliamentary procedure which help to conduct floor debate in an orderly manner. Legislators who have a good grasp of procedural rules have an advantage in debate over those who have a more limited understanding of parliamentary procedure.

8. Generally during floor debate, each side has a floor leader who plans and organizes the debate of people on his side of the issue. The floor leader is nearly always a member of the committee which considered the bill, often the chairman.

9. On some legislative issues a congressman has a fairly pronounced and one-sided constituency preference expressed to him. When this is the case, such as on a gun control bill, the congressman will tend to vote according to this constituency preference unless he has some very strong and unusual personal reasons for voting differently. Legislators hesitate to cast a vote in such a way that their reelection might be jeopardized.

10. On many other issues, the constituency preference is not so pronounced nor as one-sided. On these issues the legislator has quite a bit of leeway or discretion in

deciding how to vote. In such situations there are several factors which may help determine how the legislator votes. One is his personal judgment and past public record on the issue. He may have a well developed, publicly known position which he is unlikely to change. Another factor may be the position taken by party leaders and/or the President and the administration. Still another may be the position of an influential interest group. An interest group may be influential because of a strong base in the legislator's district. However, some interest groups are influential with a given legislator even though they may not have a base in his district. They may be a source of trusted information on the issue. Or they may have contributed generously to the member's campaign in the last election.

11. There are times when it makes sense for legislators to trade votes. If the legislator does not feel strongly about an issue and if there is no pronounced constituency preference, he may be willing to trade his vote on the issue in return for another legislator's support on an issue of major concern to the first legislator.

12. In floor debate some members stand out as being very articulate and effective. They emerge as informal leaders in the legislature.

13. In the Congress, members rarely vote along strict party lines. Rather, coalitions are formed for and against a bill with members of both parties in each coalition. Sometimes the coalitions form along ideological lines, the liberals versus the conservatives. Other times the division is along geographical lines, the sunbelt versus the midwest and northeast, or the northwest against the southwest with the rest of the country holding the balance of power. Legislators come to realize that a congressman who is his opponent on one bill may be his ally on another, and vice versa. This fact tends to moderate the sharpness of the conflict during a legislative debate.

14. Legislators need to be able to trust each other when one gives his word to a colleague that he will support a certain bill. There may be unusual circumstances in which a person has to change his position, but generally legislators can count on each other to stand by their word once they have given it.

15. Taking a head count, that is, finding out which legislators have decided to support a bill, which ones have decided to oppose it, and which ones are still undecided is a very important part of the legislative process. On a bill where support is evenly divided, there may be a great deal of pressure put on the uncommitted legislators by their colleagues, by the President or his lobbyists, or by lobbyists from organized interest groups.

16. Organized interest groups are an important part of the legislative process. They are a source of expert information which can sometimes influence a legislator. They may have made substantial contributions to a member's campaign, and in return they may expect the legislator's support on a bill of importance to the group. They may be in a position to organize a large number of voters to oppose a legislator if he votes against the group's position on a bill.

17. The President is expected to help the Congress set priorities, to decide which issues should be considered first out of the vast number of issues in need of resolution at any one time. The President generally presents what is called "the President's program," which is an indication of what the President considers to be the most urgent issues needing action quite soon.

18. Legislative issues can be very involved and complicated. It takes a great deal of time and effort to gain a thorough understanding of a complex legislative issue.

19. Congressmen have available to them staff people who can do quite a bit of

time-consuming background research on legislative issues. Congressmen depend on their legislative assistants to do this background study and to brief them before they must cast their votes or make their decisions in committee.

20. In a legislature there is a difference between a bill and a resolution. A bill makes policy if it is enacted into law. A resolution, on the other hand, is simply a declaration of how the legislators feel on a certain subject. It does not have the force of law.

APPENDIX B
Congress Decides: Simulation Bills

Agriculture Committee

SB-1.   Grain Price Supports.
SB-2.   End to Grain Price Supports.
SB-3.   Grain Reserve.

Armed Services Committee

SB-4.   Increase in Defense Budget.
SB-5.   Decrease in Defense Budget.
SB-6.   Continue M-X Intercontinental Ballistic Missile Development.
SB-7.   Stop M-X Intercontinental Ballistic Missile Development.

Energy and Natural Resources Committee

SB-8.   Natural Gas Deregulation.
SB-9.   Natural Gas Price Increase.
SB-10. Water Import from Columbia River to Colorado River.
SB-11. Moratorium on Inter-basin Water Imports.

Environment and Public Works Committee

SB-12. Tax on Air and Water Pollution.
SB-13. Requirement for Best Available Pollution Control Equipment.
SB-14. Yellowstone River Dam.

Foreign Relations Committee

SB-15. Panama Canal Treaties Ratification.
SB-16. Hard Line Toward the Soviet Union.
SR-1.   Resolution in Favor of a Policy of Detente with the Soviet Union.

Human Resources Committee

SB-17. Health Care for All Americans.
SB-18. Health Care for the Poor.
SB-19. Guaranteed Annual Income.

APPENDIX C
Congress Decides: Simulation Roles

District	Party	Coalition
Northeast	Democrat	Liberal
Pacific Northwest	Democrat	Liberal

Great Lakes	Democrat	Liberal
Prairie South	Democrat	Moderate
Desert Southwest	Democrat	Conservative
Ozark Region	Democrat	Conservative
Deep South	Democrat	Conservative
North Atlantic	Republican	Liberal
Pacific Southwest	Republican	Liberal
Great Plains	Republican	Conservative
Midwest	Republican	Moderate
Rocky Mountains	Republican	Conservative

APPENDIX D
Sample Bill and Background Information

SB-13. *Requirement for Best Available Pollution Control Equipment*

All private and public organizations whose operations create air or water pollution are required to install by 1984 the best available pollution control equipment, regardless of how costly such equipment might be.

Background Information

Proponents of this bill argue that we should reduce air and water pollution to the absolute minimum. Otherwise, they say, we face growing and unacceptable damage to the environment and to human health.

It should be pointed out, though, that equipment to reduce pollution to the maximum feasible extent is very costly. This bill would impose a tremendous financial burden on private industries and also on cities and towns which operate sewage systems. These cities and towns would not be able to afford these systems without either greatly increased taxes or user fees or substantial federal and state money. Some private companies might be forced out of business by the bill. Others would have to raise their prices.

APPENDIX E
Simulation Rating Scale

Directions: On each item circle the number which seems to you the most appropriate rating.

1. OBJECTIVES OF THE EXERCISE CLARIFIED BY INSTRUCTOR

10	9	8	7	6	5	4	3	2	1

Objectives clearly defined. / Objectives somewhat vague or indefinite. / Objectives very vague or given no attention.

2. RELATION OF SIMULATION MODEL TO REALITY

10	9	8	7	6	5	4	3	2	1

Very realistic. / Realistic enough to be somewhat informative / Completely unrealistic.

3. VALUE OF EXERCISE AS A LEARNING DEVICE

10	9	8	7	6	5	4	3	2	1

Much more valuable a learning device than reading, lectures, and discussions.

Equal to reading, lectures, and discussions as a contribution to learning.

Much less valuable than reading, lectures, and discussion.

4. PERSONAL ENJOYMENT OF EXERCISE

10	9	8	7	6	5	4	3	2	1

Very enjoyable.

Somewhat enjoyable.

Not at all enjoyable.

5. AMOUNT OF TIME SPENT IN RELATION TO THE VALUE OF THE EXERCISE

10	9	8	7	6	5	4	3	2	1

So valuable that more time should have been spent on exercise.

The allotted time was justified, but to have spent more time would not have been warranted.

Not valuable enough to justify spending so much time on the exercise.

6. AMOUNT OF TIME SPENT IN RELATION TO STATED OBJECTIVES FOR THE EXERCISE

10	9	8	7	6	5	4	3	2	1

More time than was needed to accomplish the stated objectives.

About the right amount of time to accomplish the stated objectives.

Too little time to adequately accomplish the stated objectives.

7. List five words which best describe the simulation (such as "interesting" or "boring").

8. List the things you liked about the simulation.

9. List the things you didn't like about the simulation.

10. List two or more things you learned from the simulation.

11. What changes would you suggest in the simulation?

12. Are there any additional comments you wish to make?

Chief

Marie Natoli
Emmanuel College

OBJECTIVES

1. To demonstrate the various roles a President must perform as well as the interrelationships of these roles.

2. To demonstrate the frequent conflict and incompatibility among these roles.

3. To give students a working knowledge of the various actors a President encounters in exercising his varying roles.

4. To demonstrate political party relationships
   a. between a President and the members of his own party
   b. between a President and the members of the other party

5. To provide a framework in which students will conduct a wider research project as pre-game preparation in order to realistically fulfill the roles assigned to them.

GOALS

1. The President's most immediate task is to determine—in consultation with his advisers—the shape and timing of the legislative package he will submit to Congress during his first year in office.

2. Each of the other actor's primary goal is to work towards achieving what is in his/her interests.

3. Each (interest/individual) is free to devise a program/legislation for which it may lobby at whichever level it deems appropriate.

GUIDELINES FOR THE INSTRUCTOR

1. This game is not designed to produce a clear-cut "winner." Rather, its purpose is to demonstrate the political activity involved in presidential priority setting.

2. The role of the instructor should be minimal, although a more active environment can be created if the instructor desires to introduce "surprises" towards which the participants would have to react.

3. Roles can be expanded upon in terms of both instructions as well as numbers of participants, depending upon the instructor's overall objective in using this simulation as well as upon class size.

4. Issues can be added—depending upon the instructor's overall objective in

using this simulation game as part of a wider treatment of the American Presidency.

5. Allow each participant to read the backgrounds of all other participants.

NUMBER OF PLAYERS

This particular version of "Chief" requires a minimum of 19 players.

This number, however, is arbitrary insofar as I have chosen to create that many character types. To accommodate a smaller class, it would be possible to eliminate one or some of the lesser roles. Likewise, a larger class can be even more easily accommodated by creating similarly realistic players (e.g., another Senatorial "type" perhaps; more interest groups; or, by having several students share one role (see "Actors").

PHYSICAL REQUIREMENTS AND RESTRICTIONS

1. It is desirable to isolate the President, preferably in a separate room, but if one is not available, an isolated corner of the same room will do.

2. The only actors with direct access to the President are the members of his immediate staff. All others must go through the Chief of Staff.

3. All other actors may interact freely and may enter into any agreements/relationships upon which they can mutually agree.

4. The final first year program presented by the White House cannot exceed $50 billion.

TIME

1. Actual classroom time can be limited to one 50-minute hour if necessary, but either one longer session or the continuation of the game over several class sessions is desirable.

2. Pre-game preparation must be very extensive—at least one week of outside-class time in which actors can research their appropriate role behaviors.

3. The game ends with the determination of the White House of the final legislative package it will submit to the Senate.

It is suggested that the Instructor end the game by saying: "And now on to the House of Representatives"—which will undoubtedly provide a jumping off point for discussion (during the de-briefing) of the further complexities of presidential policymaking.

ACTORS

TOM MOORE, President of the United States.

Tom Moore, a Democrat and a Senator from an Eastern state, has just been elected President of the United States following a long hard campaign in which several crucial and controversial issues were debated.

One of these issues concerned the merits and demerits of a federally-instituted job program to ease the burden of unemployment as well as to provide a first step towards reforming the U.S. welfare system. Moore was a proponent of such a program.

His opponent, BILL GRIGLEY, a middle-of-the-road Republican from the Mid-West, emphasized the need for solving the problem of unemployment, but cautioned against the cost of a federal program, and based his approach upon greater private business initiative.

A second issue had been the role of the United States abroad—politically, economically, militarily. Both Moore and Grigley had stressed the necessity of maintaining U.S. superiority militarily, as well as its role as leader of the Western world, while emphasizing that this did not mean involvement in the internal affairs of other nations.

A third issue concerned a comprehensive health care program. Moore had spent a good deal of his time on this issue and was pledged to its realization, just as he had stressed his commitment to formulating a comprehensive energy program to deal with one of the nation's most pressing problems.

The campaign had found Moore and his Republican opponent alternating for top place in the public opinion polls. By election day in November, none of the pollsters was willing to predict a winner. The newscasting went well into the night. Finally, at 6 a.m., ABC was calling Moore the victor. But both candidates were more cautious. Grigley did not offer his concession speech until 9 a.m., with Moore's victory statement following closely on its heels.

The final popular vote margin for Moore was a mere 150,000 votes, although he was significantly ahead in the Electoral College tally.

The elections also found a Democratic House and Senate in office, and two-thirds of the governors' offices were controlled by Democrats. But Moore had run well behind his party nationwide.

Inauguration Day was indeed a happy one for the Democrats.

But now the President faced a difficult four years. He knew he would particularly face a tough time in the Senate where many members of his own party had reservations about his ability to lead, and where he anticipated a tough battle on a treaty he planned to submit for Senate confirmation.

The President's most immediate task is to determine—in consultation with his advisers—the shape and timing of the legislative package he will submit to Congress during his first year in office.

White House Staff (roles can be added or eliminated, depending upon the number of class participants):

JACK GREEN. As the President's unofficial Chief of Staff, Jack is responsible for overseeing the extensive White House staff, as well as for serving as a general adviser to the President.

Jack had been the President's campaign manager during the past election, so he is well-versed with the complexities of the issues in the recent election and knows that the President has to draw a balance between treading cautiously and forging a legislative record which will be an asset during the next Presidential election, in which Bill Grigley is undoubtedly planning to make a second bid for the Presidency.

JOHN CAREY, Jack Green's assistant.

MARGARET DACY, Presidential aide, and the only woman on the top White House staff.

(Note to Instructor: Be careful to provide appropriate background in creating additional White House staff.)

Senators:

MIKE BELLEN, Senate Majority Leader and Texas Democrat.
    As a 25-year incumbent of the legislature (21 years of which have been spent in the Senate), Bellen has been the Senate's top leader for the past six years. He knows that he represents not only his own constituency of a Southern state, but the wider constituency of Senators, who have selected him as Majority Leader.
    Of the 66 Democrats in the Senate, he knows that 41 believe that the federal government should institute a job program. Of these 41, 20 feel (with varying degrees of commitment) that this program should be tied in with welfare reform; the remaining 12 feel it should not. Twenty-three Democratic Senators are opposed to the program (12 of them staunchly). Twelve Democratic Senators are uncommitted.
    As for the role of the U.S. abroad, 24 liberal Democratic Senators feel it should be curtailed. Twenty conservative Democratic Senators feel it must be expanded. Twenty-six are undecided.
    And on the issue of a comprehensive health program, the breakdown finds liberal Democrats supporting a strong program with not only provisions regarding catastrophic illness, but provisions guaranteeing every American's right to preventive care as well. With some slight variations, this faction would incorporate cost containment for both doctors and hospitals. The more conservative of the Democratic Senators realize that some sort of health legislation is mandated, but would opt for a more modified program which would guard against the financial dangers of catastrophic illness, but which would involve high users' costs and which would assume a laissez-faire attitude toward the medical profession.

RODNEY BYRNES, Minority Leader and Senator from a Mid-Western state.
    Byrnes leads a party which is sorely splintered among a staunchly conservative wing (approximately 12 Senators, depending upon the issue), and equally liberal wing (approximately 10 Senators, depending upon the issue), and the remainder hovering in the middle, sometimes voting with the conservatives

and sometimes with the liberals (Bill Grigley is the unofficial spokesperson for this group of Senators), but who usually attempt to achieve some sort of compromise in order to maintain a sense of unity within the party.

Byrnes knows that his principal task is to achieve the party unity so essential to success against the opposition. He knows, too, that (in consideration of the close election) his party's candidate might very well have won the Presidency had the Republican Party not been so divided in the past election.

BOB SMITHERINE, a Southern Democrat.

AL JORDAN, an Eastern Democrat from a state with large urban minorities.

JOAN KELLOGG, a Republican liberal from the West Coast who has just won election on a strong woman's plank.

BILL WILLIAMS, a middle-of-the-road Republican from the Mid-West who had an eye on the party presidential nomination.

Interest Groups:

EDWARD REARDON, Chairman of the Chamber of Commerce.

RITA KAHIL, President of the National Organization of Women (NOW).

Dr. ARTHUR PACE, President of the American Medical Association (AMA).

GEORGE NICEY, President of the AFL-CIO.

CITY MAYORS (at least one individual, but more are desirable).

JOINT CHIEFS OF STAFF (at least one individual, but more are desirable).

EDUCATION COMMUNITY.

BLACK COMMUNITY.

General Interest Instructions: Each interest is free to devise its own program/ legislation for which it may lobby at whichever level(s) it deems appropriate.

(Note to Instructor: Each of the above may also be represented by lobbyists for their cause. This will provide flexibility with which to accommodate varying class sizes.)

DE-BRIEFING

Some suggested questions for exploration:

1. Were the roles depicted realistic? (a) Were any actors you might find in the real world left out?

2. Were the programs suggested likely to be suggested in the real world political arena?

3. What are your impressions of the roles performed by a President in formulating a legislative package?

4. What political constraints might a President encounter in formulating a legislative package?

5. What is the effect of the nature of the American party system upon how a President behaves?

6. What is the role of interest groups in Presidential politics and priority setting?

7. What roles besides those demonstrated in this simulation would you imagine a President may have to play?

8. What kinds of incompatibilities might occur among these roles?

Crisis Decision-Making: The World from Washington

Louis E. Leopold
The Pennsylvania State University, Altoona Campus

Course/Level: Courses: International Politics, U.S. Foreign Policy at the undergraduate level. Level: Models of the Decision Process approached through Individual Decision-Making, Negotiating, Bargaining and Crisis Decision-Making Processes.

Number of Players: 16-40.

Roles: Four decision-making teams.
   Team A: "WSAG"—Washington Special Action Group (5-10 players) (Bureaucratic Departmental and Institutional Representatives).
   Team B: "WAS"—Washington Ancient-Analytical Strategists (3-10 players) (wise men/rational decision makers).
   Team C: "JCOS"—Joint Chiefs of Staff (3-8 players).
   Team D: "WPOL"—Washington Politicos (4-10 players) (Top Congressional, Party and White House political leadership).
   The "Exec"—The President (and the Vice-President?) (1-2 players) (some instructors may wish to play God).

Timing: Two to three class periods; may be continued if the same crisis is tied in with other elements of the course.

Stages: (1) Crisis briefing, (2) Actual team decision-making, (3) Presentation of team decisions to the President, (4) Oval Office team debriefing, (5) The President Decides(?).

Physical Facilities: Minimum—one large room that can be subdivided for the separate team meetings. Ideal—separate meeting rooms for each team.

Preparation: Prior to or during simulation and debriefing period, exposure to some of the basic concepts and models of crisis decision-making. A detailed briefing on the actual "crisis" itself with a "handout" to supplement the briefing officer's (instructor) crisis presentation, which should include maps, diagrams, etc.

Special Materials: (a) Name and position identification tags; (b) Role background sheets for most players, suggesting their special interests, needs and prior commitments; (c) Crisis development dispatches for specific roles; (d) Crisis decision forms, including individual and team needs and interests—options to achieve these and final recommendations and justifications, along with likely response.

Narrative: The briefing officer presents the class with a foreign policy international security crisis scenario (it helps if other course materials have touched on the region involved). In the spring of 1971 we ran an India-Pakistan Crisis. More recently we used a post-Tito Yugoslavian crisis. Currently, it is a revolt in the desert. The rebels seize Mecca and Medina. The hard-pressed royal forces still hold Riyadh and the oil fields. The royal government has sent an urgent request for all-out military help in repelling the PLO- and Iraqi-supported rebels.

Each of the four decision-making teams has been asked by the President to give him its best judgment on what can be done. They are to spell out basic U.S. needs and interests in the conflict; what options are available to best secure them; their specific recommendations, and the likely outcomes.

Team A, chaired by the Assistant to the President for National Security Affairs, and modeled after the Washington Special Action Group, is programmed to view the crisis from their respective bureaucratic institutional perspectives. Depending on the number of players, the following should be represented: the Secretary of State, Secretaries of Defense and Energy, the Director of the CIA, the Chairman of the Joint Chiefs, the U.S. Ambassador to the UN, and, if available, the Director of the U.S. Information Agency, the Assistant Secretaries of State for Near East and South Asian Affairs, etc.

Team B is designed as a mix of "wise men" and scientific analysts who are free to make rational decisions without current bureaucratic involvement. They could include people like: the Directors of Brookings and Rand, Henry

Kissinger, Dean Rusk, Elliot Richardson, Herman Kahn, Joseph Sisco, et al. They are meeting unofficially, informally, and the very existence of the group is a secret.

Team C is made up of the Joint Chiefs of Staff, who may be augmented by the Marine Corps Commandant and by involved area and unit commanders—U.S. 6th Fleet, U.S. Strategic Reserve Force, and the like. Team C will be provided with data sheets on available U.S. forces and potential friendly and unfriendly forces in the area, as well as staff scenarios.

Team D is made up of key political party and Congressional leaders—the Speaker of the House and the Majority Leader of the Senate. From the White House staff, the Assistant to the President Jordan Hamm, the Press Secretary P. L. Jody and, as available, Special Representative for Trade Negotiations Ambassador S. Strauss Roberts, Chairman of the Senate Foreign Relations Committee, etc.

Each team will prepare a final recommendation with justifications. One member will present it when called to the Oval Office. The President, assisted by his Assistant for National Security Affairs, his Press Secretary, his Assistant Jordan Hamm, and any other members that he requests, will question the presenters and the recommendations, examine the written reports, and, in due course, announce U.S. policy and its justification.

As part of the final debriefing, team members may question the President as to his rationale. The various recommendations will be considered in light of the currently popular models of decision making and decision "rules."

Collective Bargaining in Public Higher Education Simulation

Dennis J. O'Donnell
University of Montana

Peter H. Koehn and Robert E. Eagle
University of Montana

1. *Subject Matter:* Faculty collective bargaining in a state university.

2. *Courses and Levels for Which Simulation is Appropriate:* This simulation is appropriate for upper-level undergraduate and graduate level courses in economics or public administration which deal with public employee labor relations and collective bargaining. It was used jointly in two classes at the University of Montana—a graduate-level political science class in public personnel administration taught by Professor Koehn and a class for upper level undergraduate and graduate students in economics on collective bargaining taught by Professor O'Donnell. Two separate simulations were conducted

concurrently, each involving students from both classes. Professor O'Donnell plans to run a similar simulation next year involving an economics class and a business administration class simulating collective bargaining in the private sector.

3. *Number of Participants:*

Minimum:	12 per simulation
Maximum:	16 per simulation
Optimum:	14 per simulation

4. *Length of Time for Simulation:* Minimum: In a three- or four-credit course, five weeks for the simulation itself plus three to four weeks for preparation.

Maximum: In a three- or four-credit course, two complete quarters or one entire semester could usefully be devoted to the simulation.

Optimum: Ten weeks for simulation itself plus three to four weeks for preparation.

5. *Schedule of Activities:* Individual students on both the union and the management teams are assigned specific subject areas on which they prepare preliminary proposals. These proposals are then brought before the respective negotiating teams which coordinate the preliminary proposals and designate final proposals and overall bargaining strategy.

Next comes the first face-to-face meeting of the two bargaining teams. At this meeting, proposals may be exchanged and ground rules determined. Then, several days later, there is a second meeting of the two teams at which counterproposals may be exchanged. Following this exchange of counterproposals, each bargaining team meets separately in caucus to prepare for the negotiating sessions.

There are four formal negotiating sessions spread over four weeks. The first three sessions may last from three to five hours. The last session may last longer, as much as seven hours, depending on what kind of deadline is established to conclude the session with or without a negotiated agreement. During this four-week period there are also other informal meetings taking place. Subcommittees of representatives of each team may meet to hash out the issues in a preliminary way. Students acting as the state Board of Regents (in addition to their regular roles as members of a bargaining team) also hold meetings. Considerable student time is spent in out-of-class preparation during this negotiating period.

When the final negotiating session has been concluded, the Board of Regents meets to approve or disapprove the contract, if a contract has in fact been negotiated. Following this action, the union class meets separately to vote on whether or not to ratify the contract, assuming the Board of Regents has approved it.

The faculty vote on ratification is the last step in the simulation. Following this vote, a class period is devoted to a discussion and evaluation of the simulation.

FIGURE 1.
Structure of Bargaining

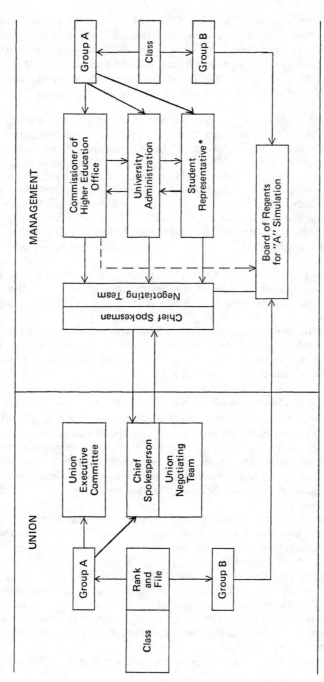

*Included under Montana law as part of management bargaining team.

6. *Required Physical Facilities:* One room with a long table and comfortable chairs is needed for each simulation. Two additional rooms are needed for each simulation so that each bargaining team will have a private place in which to caucus. Since the negotiating sessions last for several hours, it is very helpful if there is a coffee shop or other facility where beverages may be obtained. A clock should also be available which can be seen by the negotiators.

7. *Student Preparation for Simulation:* It is important that students have some basic information about labor law, public personnel systems, labor relations, and collective bargaining before they begin the simulation itself. Some of this information may be acquired in prior courses which are a prerequisite for the course in which the simulation takes place. Or this information can be covered at the beginning of the course through readings, lectures, and discussions. Outside resource persons can be brought in to enrich this preparation period. For example, when these courses were being offered at the University of Montana, a professional negotiator for the American Federation of Teachers was available and was brought in as a guest speaker in a joint workshop in which both classes participated.

A short mini-simulation can be used to give students a first taste of what bargaining sessions are like. A limited number of issues, as few as one and as many as five, can be used in a brief bargaining session to provide this preliminary experience.

Students should also be given a bibliography of materials which they can consult before and during the simulation to obtain further information on collective bargaining in general as well as model contracts and contracts used in public higher educational institutions.

8. *Special Materials Needed:* Name tags are helpful, especially in the first face-to-face meetings. Each student should be given a list of the names, simulation roles, addresses and phone numbers, and hours of availability of every participant in the simulation. These lists help facilitate the out-of-class meetings that are necessary throughout the bargaining period. Typing and duplicating facilities are also needed so that students may exchange proposals both within their bargaining teams and between the two teams.

9. *Other Features:* When it was run at the University of Montana, this simulation involved students from two classes—a 300-level economics class and a 500- (graduate) level class in public administration. Students from the economics class played the part of the faculty union bargaining team, while students in the public administration class played the part of the management bargaining team. A small number of undergraduate political science students also participated, playing the role of student representatives who, under Montana law, are involved in faculty bargaining proceedings, sitting on the management side and participating in the management caucuses but having no vote on the final contract.

Because of the number of students involved, a total of 39 in the two classes, two separate simulations were run concurrently. The two instructors collaborated in planning and administering the simulation. One worked with each simulation, and they shifted each session. Having students from two different classes meant that most of the students from one class (and bargaining team) didn't know the students in the other class (the opposing bargaining team) until they met for the first time face-to-face in the simulation. It is not necessary to have two different classes involved in a collective bargaining simulation. Such simulations have been run successfully by Professor O'Donnell using students from only one class.

At the time this simulation was conducted, real life faculty collective bargaining was just getting underway at the University of Montana. The situation at the University of Montana was used as an empirical referent for the students, but they were not bound to any of the specific proposals put forth by either real life bargaining team. The fact that in the simulation the contract to be negotiated was a first contract allowed students to deal with a variety of issues and to have a great deal of flexibility for negotiating. On the other hand, it might have proved easier for the bargaining teams to reach a contract in the simulation if a second contract had been being negotiated. Most of the other collective bargaining simulations with which the authors are familiar deal with second contracts.

It is a real challenge to structure a collective bargaining process for a simulation because the bargaining process itself is so loosely structured. In comparison, say, with a legislature, a collective bargaining process is much less strictly defined and institutionalized, with many of the bargaining procedures themselves subject to negotiation in the real world. The simulation itself therefore needs to allow considerable flexibility, but at the same time it must be sufficiently structured so that it will fit into the available time. One important feature of the University of Montana simulation was the reduction of the bargainable issues from several dozen potential issues to a list of eight. Probably the most difficult issue for the students to handle was the financial issue. Even though the students playing these roles had some public finance background, and even though they were provided with ample data, this was a difficult area because of its complexity and because only simulated legislative budget guidelines could be established.

There were some aspects of the simulation that were not clearly delineated at the beginning by the instructors. Most of the rules of the simulation were given verbally by each instructor separately to his own class. It would be better to have as many of the rules as possible written in a common manual. Also, rules should be presented at a joint meeting of both classes.

Where the structure of the simulation was not clear, students attempted to bargain with the instructors over the structure of the simulation in order to gain perceived advantages for their team. In most cases, the instructors realized that whatever decision they reached on a disputed rule or structural feature would be viewed as an advantage for one side or the other. The more the structure of the simulation can be firmly established ahead of time, the less need there will be to make such structural decisions while the simulation is in progress. But, given the loose structure of the collective bargaining process itself and the unique variables at work each time a new set of negotiating teams sits down at the bargaining table, it is probably inevitable that the instructor(s) will have to make some decisions on rules and structure while the simulation is in progress. In making these decisions, there probably will be a tension between approximating the real world on the one hand and fulfilling pedagogical objectives and making the simulation exercise manageable on the other.

TABLE 1
Student Evaluations of the Simulations
(Means on scale from a low of 1 to a high of 10)

	Class	
Item Being Rated	Political Science 592 (N=15)	Economics 34 (N=13)
Objectives of the exercise clarified by instructor	5.33	8.00
Relation of simulation model to reality	4.93	7.92
Value of exercise as a learning device	6.00	9.54
Personal enjoyment of exercise	5.33	8.23
Amount of time spent in relation to the value of the exercise*	3.67	6.69
Amount of time spent in relation to stated objectives for the exercise**	4.20	6.15

*On this item a rating of 3.67 indicates the simulation was not valuable enough to justify spending so much time on it. A rating of 6.69 indicates that the allotted time was justified, but to have spent more time would not have been warranted.

**The optimal rating on this item would be 5.50. On the other items the optimal rating would be 10.00.

10. *Evaluation:* A structured rating form (copy attached as Appendix A) was used to facilitate student evaluations of the simulations. The ratings for the two University of Montana classes are shown in Table 1 above. The ratings of the students in the economics class, mostly undergraduates, were predominantly positive in nature. The rating on value as a learning device is one of the highest ratings on this item that Professor Eagle has seen in over two dozen simulations in which this rating scale has been used. A typical comment from the economics class was, "It was terrific."

The ratings from the political science class, mostly graduate students, were more moderate and mixed. Some ratings from this group were strongly positive, but others were markedly negative. In the experience of Professor Eagle with other simulations at different levels of instruction, it is not uncommon for graduate students to be more critical of such exercises than are undergraduates. Graduate students are more experienced and have higher standards of expectation, generally, than do undergraduate students. Graduate students tend to be more involved in school, with more riding on each class than undergraduates, and may more intensely feel the frustrations inherent in the bargaining process.

A common complaint from both classes was that the simulation required too much time for a three- or four-credit course. Another frequent criticism was a certain lack of coordination between the two instructors. Some felt that the instructors, in conducting unfair labor practice hearings, tended to be biased toward their own students rather than objective in their rulings.

The positive comments were many from both classes. Students felt that this simulation gave them much more depth of understanding of the collective bargaining process than they would have obtained without the simulation.

The importance of student personalities was a feature of the simulations mentioned by many students. Some mentioned this factor in a positive vein, noting that it was valuable to see the impact of different personalities on a bargaining process. Others made negative comments about the personalities involved, feeling that in some cases personality clashes developed that were detrimental not only to the simulated bargaining process but to the learning process in general.

On the whole the student ratings were moderately to strongly positive. It is interesting that the item receiving the highest rating in both groups was the value of the exercise as a learning device. This rating reinforces the conclusion of the authors that the simulation was indeed a valuable learning experience for most of the students. To be sure, there were some problems with the simulation as there are with any simulation the first time it is tried. Some of these problems are mentioned below. But the authors conclude that the exercise was on balance a useful way to teach students about collective bargaining in public higher education and they look forward to using similar simulations in the future.

Grading. In the Political Science 592 class, the grade for each student was made up of three parts. A peer evaluation of the student's performance in the simulation, using the form attached as Appendix B, counted as 40 percent of the grade. An evaluation of simulation performance by the instructor counted 20 percent. The final 40 percent of the student's grade came from the instructor's evaluation of a paper which was due about a week after the simulation ended. Students were asked to present in this paper their ideal proposal in their area of issue responsibility and a justification of this proposal based on the literature in personnel administration; an account of what happened to this proposal during each phase of the bargaining process (including internal management negotiations) and why the student felt he could live with what was finally agreed to at the table or happened as a result of failure to reach an agreement; and an assessment of the team's bargaining performance with reference to the literature on collective bargaining strategy and tactics.

In the Economics 324 class, there was a midterm examination which counted 25 percent of the course grade. There were also assignments to prepare evaluations of National Labor Relations Board decisions regarding good-faith bargaining and interference with union activities as well as an arbitration case. These written case studies together constituted 25 percent of the student's grade. The remaining 50 percent of the course grade was a paper on the simulation. In this paper, students were asked to define the area in which they had responsibility, both their issue area and their position in the union; to describe and justify their initial proposal with reference to the literature; to describe how their proposal was altered by their own team in the development of a team bargaining strategy, including the relative priority of their issue; to assess the team's bargaining strategy with reference to the literature; to keep a journal of the bargaining process to show at each stage of the negotiations what happened to their proposal; and to do a critical evaluation of the bargaining done by their team with emphasis on self-criticism—where they did well and what they did wrong, relating their goals to their ultimate achievements in the simulation.

11. *Narrative:* The instructors decided to use a simulation because they felt it would be particularly appropriate as a training device for collective bargaining. The experience of participating in a series of simulated negotiations can lead students to an understanding of the bargaining process that is difficult to achieve through other teaching methods.

The decision to involve two different classes from two disciplines in the simulation emerged for several reasons. First, the instructors of the two classes knew each other quite well and the idea of collaborating on the simulation appealed to them personally. Second, both classes were scheduled to deal with issues in collective bargaining in the public sector, so the subject matter in each class was appropriate for the simulation. Third, the instructors thought it would be useful and realistic to involve the two different classes in such a way that students from one class would face students from another class across the bargaining table. This arrangement would encourage feelings of group solidarity within the bargaining teams and would mean that members of opposing teams would start out without knowing each other in most cases.

A key element in the simulation was the decision to use the current real-life situation at the University of Montana as the empirical referent for the simulation. Negotiations for a first contract were just getting underway between the University Teachers Union, an affiliate of the American Federation of Teachers, and representatives of the university administration, the state Board of Regents, and the Commissioner of Higher Education. Using the current real-life situation meant that students already were familiar with a good deal of the background information that would be needed for the simulation. If a hypothetical university had been used as a model, it would have been necessary for the instructors to develop an elaborate manual describing in detail numerous facets of the hypothetical university. There would likewise have been a need to develop elaborate background information had the simulation dealt with another public agency such as a police department. In addition, by using the real university as the empirical referent, further information was available from a number of nearby and accessible sources, although some effort was necessary on the part of the students to acquire such data.

The simulation exercise was designed so that each student had a specific role and also had individual responsibility for one of the issues to be bargained which related to the responsibilities of their role. The roles in the simulation were as follows:

Management Team

Chief Spokesperson (member of staff of Commissioner of Higher Education)
Academic Vice President of the University
Budget Officer of the University
Legal Counselor and Equal Employment Opportunity Officer for the
    Commissioner of Higher Education
University President
Commissioner of Higher Education
Legal Counselor for the University
Student Representative

Faculty Union Team

Executive Committee
    President and Legal Counsel
    Vice President
    Secretary
    Treasurer
    Elected Chief Spokesperson
Rank and file

Each member of the faculty union team represented a particular academic department or school in the university.

Issues to be bargained were designated as union issues, management issues, or joint issues as indicated below:

Issues to be Bargained

Union issues
    union security
    grievance procedures

Management issues
    management rights and faculty/student involvement in management
    performance appraisal

Joint issues
    salaries and fringe benefits
    layoffs
    tenure and academic freedom
    student-faculty ratios and workload

Roles and issue responsibilities were assigned early in the quarter so that students would have time to prepare for the simulation. In addition to these primary roles and responsibilities, there were also some secondary responsibilities and roles. For each of the simulations, a five-member State Board of Regents was chosen to oversee and give feedback to the management team. The Board of Regents members who supervised management team A were chosen from the other simulation group, and vice versa. On each Board of Regents there were members from both classes. Regents were chosen on the basis of written statements submitted by students indicating what orientation they would have if chosen for the Board.

Each union bargaining team was ultimately accountable to the entire membership of the Economics 324 class, representing the whole faculty, who were given a chance to vote on the final contract. See Figure 1 for a diagram of the lines of accountability for each bargaining team.

If only one simulation were being run, there would not be a second group from which to draw members of the Board of Regents and additional faculty members to vote on the contract. In a single simulation, the instructor could act as the Board of Regents, providing feedback to the management bargaining team. Or the simulation could be run without a Board of Regents, but this omission would involve a loss of valuable feedback for the management bargaining team. A third alternative would be to have students in another class act as the Board of Regents. In a class on state government, public finance, or the politics of higher education, all of which are taught from time to time at the University of Montana, it would be appropriate to have the students in the class take some of their time to evaluate and respond to the bargaining proposals being put forth by the management bargaining team in the collective bargaining simulation class. Interaction could be in writing or in person. Professor Eagle has used this approach by having students in a class on interest groups act as lobbyists for a legislative simulation being conducted in another class.

It would also be possible and to some extent desirable for some other outside group such as a volunteer group of faculty members or another class to respond to the union's position on the negotiated contract by acting as the whole faculty to approve or reject the contract. The final faculty vote could, of course, be eliminated, but the instructors who ran this simulation consider this final faculty vote to be an important incentive to the union bargaining team to reach a contract that is acceptable not only to the union membership but to the faculty as a whole.

There is one other set of roles to be filled in the simulation. These roles relate to the functions of mediation, arbitration, fact finding, and hearing appeals of unfair labor practices. In the simulation at the University of Montana, the two instructors acted as the state Board of Personnel Appeals and in that capacity they heard two appeals of unfair labor practices during the course of the simulation. A problem arose by having the two instructors fill this role. Students tended to perceive the instructor in their class as a champion for their team in regard to the unfair labor practice disputes. Some students felt that the instructors' decisions as members of the Board of Personnel Appeals were in fact biased toward their own classes. If there is an outside person or group of persons well versed on labor law who could act as the Board of Personnel Appeals in hearing unfair labor practice cases, this would eliminate the problem of possible instructor bias in playing this role.

The functions of mediating, arbitrating, and fact finding were also played by the instructors. Much fact finding was done by the instructors during the simulation, some by one instructor alone and some by both of them. This basically involved clarification of fact and law for the students. In this simulation a request for mediation or arbitration did not arise, although both groups discussed it seriously. Had it come up, it would have been handled by the instructor not presently in the room. The students did not know which instructor it would have been. Had they known ahead of time which instructor it would be, students from one class may have perceived a potential advantage in seeking mediation or arbitration.

The question arose as to how much help and advice the instructors should provide to students while the simulation is in progress. The instructors tried to keep from giving one team any information or advice while bargaining at the table or in subcommittee was in progress on the grounds that the students should be prepared for all contingencies. But it was difficult to refrain in all cases from answering questions that the students raised, particularly when the progress of bargaining would be delayed by refusing to provide the information. If such questions do arise, it is important that the instructor(s) make sure that both sides in fact do not know the answer to the question and both agree that it is necessary to have the information immediately before they answer it. If one side has the information and the other side doesn't, then to answer the question would help one side. If the instructor is going to answer a question, it should be done so that both sides receive the same information at the same time. This can be accomplished by providing the information to both teams while they are together at the bargaining table.

The function of arbitration would best be performed by an outsider rather than the instructors since in arbitration the arbitrator himself makes a decision that is likely to have a substantial effect on the final contract outcome. The instructor tends to become too closely involved with one side to render an impartial and painless decision. However, the functions of mediation and fact finding, which do not involve such critical decisions, can be played by the instructors.

If the simulation is being run in one class with only one instructor, then the instructor may be able to play the roles of appeals board, mediator, arbitrator, and fact finder without the same problems of possible bias that come up if two classes with two instructors are involved. Regardless of who is performing these functions in the simulation, it is important that whoever acts in these capacities have a good grasp of the labor law applicable to collective bargaining at the institution and in the state being used as a model in the simulation. The person or persons performing these functions should have available to them during the simulation the state and national statutes regarding labor law and also *Labor Law Course,* 22nd edition (Commerce Clearing House, Inc.), a comprehensive reference manual that is quite helpful in locating quickly the applicable provisions of state and national law for a specific controversy that may arise during the simulation.

Once the roles and issue responsibilities have been assigned, students begin working individually on their preliminary proposals. They consult literature cited in the bibliography provided by the instructors, including model contracts and examples of actual contracts, in developing their preliminary proposals. Then the bargaining teams meet as groups to develop an overall set of priorities and a general bargaining strategy and to make appropriate modifications of the individual proposals.

Before the simulation negotiating sessions begin, if two classes are involved both should meet together for a joint session to go over the rules. One problem that came up in the University of Montana simulation was that each instructor separately gave the rules to his own class. There were some differences in understanding in the two classes as to precisely what the rules were. This confusion led to some avoidable problems in the simulation itself.

In the first face-to-face meeting of the bargaining teams, there is an exchange of preliminary proposals. There should be a clear understanding ahead of time as to whether both teams will be presenting proposals at this meeting or whether only the union proposals will be put forward or whether the entire subject of the order and timing of the exchange will be negotiated at the first meeting. Also in this first session there is a determination of the ground rules for the negotiating sessions, including negotiation over the order in which the various issues will be discussed.

After several days, a second meeting is held to exchange counter-proposals. This meeting can be fairly short. After the exchange of counter-proposals, each bargaining team meets separately in caucus to prepare for the negotiating sessions. The team's overall set of priorities and general strategy should be refined in these caucus meetings.

If two classes are involved and if they do not meet at the same time, it may be necessary to schedule the negotiating sessions at a time other than the regular class meetings. In the University of Montana simulation the negotiating sessions were scheduled one evening a week for four weeks. The first three sessions were scheduled to run from 6:30 to 10 p.m., and the final session was set for 6:30 p.m. to midnight. Most sessions actually ran longer than the scheduled time.

The students on the two bargaining teams run the show completely once the negotiating sessions begin. The instructors are present as observers and are available to fill prearranged roles if the need arises. But the students are in charge of the schedule for negotiating. The two teams decide on when they wish to break and go into caucuses and when they will reconvene to resume bargaining.

For pedagogical purposes, there is a requirement that each student be given some time at the bargaining table to discuss his or her individual issue area. This is a departure from real life bargaining where there is more of a tendency to rely on one chief spokesperson to do most of the talking.

Students are allowed to meet as subcommittees with their counterparts from the opposite bargaining team for a preliminary exchange of positions or sidecar bargaining if this is agreed to by both sides when the rules governing bargaining are negotiated. Some subcommittee meetings were held outside of regularly scheduled class time and they proved useful in working toward resolution of the issues and in expanding student involvement in bargaining.

There was considerable out-of-class preparation involved for students during the simulation. Some students complained that the work load was excessive. If more than four weeks were allowed for the simulation this problem would not be as great. It is estimated that some students put in over 200 hours in total time devoted to the course, particularly some in the Political Science 592 class, which was a four-credit, one-quarter course in which normally about 120 hours of time would be a reasonable expectation (two hours out of class for every hour in class). Students in the Economics 324 class also put in a great deal of time, although there were more of them and the work could be spread around a little more than in the political science class. Students in the economics class also complained that the work expected was excessive for their course, which was only for three credits.

As was mentioned above, two unfair labor practice charges came up during the simulation. One of these was during the last negotiating session and a quick decision had to be reached to keep the simulation going.

In the two University of Montana simulations, a contract was reached by one set of teams, but the other set of teams failed to reach a contract even when the most drastic of the simulation consequences were imposed. This simulation self-destructed about 1:20 a.m. when the union was decertified and the university was permanently closed, and the remnants were distributed among the other units in the state university system.

There needs to be a set of consequences that take place in the simulation if a contract is not reached by a certain time during the final negotiating session. These consequences can involve things such as a strike by the union, exhaustion of the union strike fund, loss of public support for the strike, and, as a final drastic consequence, decertification of the union. Consequences to management could include a breakdown of support from other branches of government for the management position, a planned drop in student attendance in classes, adjournment of the legislature without any extra money coming to the university, a drop in student enrollment, faculty leaving to take jobs elsewhere, and finally, closure of the university. These consequences should be arranged as a series of deadlines so that the cost of not reaching a contract agreement is progressively increased for both the union and the management bargaining teams.

The purpose of the constraints is to compress time to induce a return to bargaining in cases of impass, or failure to reach a final contract. The students must be induced to take these simulated consequences "seriously" in order to produce the desired effect. This proved to be difficult in the session which failed to reach a final contract. Due to the late hour and the exhaustion of the list of consequences without a final agreement, the bargaining effort was abandoned for this group. This result did not appear to reduce the value of the learning experience for this group. It only intensified their frustrations and clearly illustrated the pitfalls of errors in overall bargaining strategy to both classes.

At various times during the simulation the management teams met with their respective Boards of Regents to get feedback on their negotiating positions. The Board of Regents had to approve the final contract, so it had considerable power in dealing with the management bargaining team in the simulation. There was a problem, though, in that if there was a need for a meeting with the Board of Regents for one group, the students playing the roles of the Board of Regents had to be taken out of their own negotiating session in the other simulation. For this reason it would be helpful if someone not directly involved in either simulation could play the part of the Board of Regents.

If a contract is reached, and if the Board of Regents approves it, the contract then goes before the entire faculty for approval or rejection. The whole Economics 324 class performed the function of voting for the entire faculty, but this function could be played by some other person or group.

In each class there was a final class period after the conclusion of the simulation in which discussion and evaluation of the simulation was done. Papers were assigned in both classes, as described above under the section on grading. These papers proved to be a valuable exercise of reflection and self-criticism on the part of the students, and they provided valuable information about the simulation to the instructors.

APPENDIX A
Simulation Rating Scale

Directions: On each item circle the number which seems to you the most appropriate rating.

1. OBJECTIVES OF THE EXERCISE CLARIFIED BY INSTRUCTOR

10	9	8	7	6	5	4	3	2	1

Objective clearly defined.　　　　Objective somewhat vague　　Objective very vague
　　　　　　　　　　　　　　　　or indefinite.　　　　　　or given no attention.

2. RELATION OF SIMULATION MODEL TO REALITY

10	9	8	7	6	5	4	3	2	1

Very realistic.　　　　　　　　　Realistic enough to be　　　Completely
　　　　　　　　　　　　　　　　somewhat informative.　　unrealistic.

3. VALUE OF EXERCISE AS A LEARNING DEVICE

10	9	8	7	6	5	4	3	2	1

Much more valuable as a　　　　Equal to reading, lectures,　　Much less valuable
learning device than reading,　　and discussions as a con-　　than reading, lectures
lectures, and discussions.　　　tribution to learning.　　　and discussion.

4. PERSONAL ENJOYMENT OF EXERCISE

10	9	8	7	6	5	4	3	2	1

Very enjoyable.　　　　　　　　Somewhat enjoyable.　　　Not at all enjoyable.

5. AMOUNT OF TIME SPENT IN RELATION TO THE VALUE OF THE EXERCISE

10	9	8	7	6	5	4	3	2	1

So valuable that more time should have been spent on the exercise.

The allotted time was justified, but to have spent more time would not have been warranted.

Not valuable enough to justify spending so much time on the exercise.

6. AMOUNT OF TIME SPENT IN RELATION TO STATED OBJECTIVES FOR THE EXERCISE

10	9	8	7	6	5	4	3	2	1

More time than was needed to accomplish the stated objectives.

About the right amount of time to accomplish the stated objectives.

Too little time to adequately accomplish the stated objectives.

7. List five words which best describe the simulation (such as "interesting" or "boring").

8. List the things you liked about the simulation.

9. List the things you didn't like about the simulation.

10. List two or more things you learned from the simulation.

11. What changes would you suggest in the simulation?

12. Are there any additional comments you wish to make?

APPENDIX B
Peer Evaluation Form Used in Political Science 592

NAME: _____

Criteria	+ A −		+ B −		+ C −		+ D −	
Depth of preparation in area of responsibility								
Clarity and organization of presentation								
Ability to formulate consensus and/or compromise positions								
Persuasiveness								
Creativity								
Overall effectiveness								

Krause v. Rhodes:
The Kent State Civil Trial Simulation

Thomas R. Hensley
Kent State University

Krause v. Rhodes is a simulation based upon a federal district court civil trial stemming from the May 4, 1970 shootings at Kent State University. While the simulation deals with a specific trial, the format of the simulation can be readily adapted to any criminal or civil trial for which a trial transcript is available. The simulation has been used at Kent State University primarily in an upper-division undergraduate course on the judicial process, but it could also be utilized in a constitutional law course on civil liberties.

The simulation involves students as lawyers, plaintiffs, defendants, witnesses, and jurors in a civil trial to determine if Ohio Governor James Rhodes and various Ohio National Guard officers and enlisted men are liable for damages to the nine wounded students and the parents of the four students killed on May 4th. The foundation of the simulation is the 1975 federal district court civil trial in which the jury voted 9-3 that none of the defendants was liable for damages. This decision was subsequently overturned by the Sixth Circuit Court of Appeals on the grounds that the trial judge had improperly handled a threat to a juror during the trial. The retrial commenced in December, 1978, but in January of 1979 an out-of-court settlement was reached in which the plaintiffs received $675,000 paid by the state of Ohio and a letter of regret signed by all of the defendants. In the trial simulation, student lawyers for the plaintiffs and defendants elicit testimony from students in the roles of witnesses, seeking to convince the student jurors to decide in favor of their respective clients. The purposes of the simulation are three-fold: (1) to provide insights into the processes of the American judicial system, (2) to develop knowledge about the legal issues associated with the trial, and (3) to enhance understanding of the events surrounding the May 4th shootings.

The specific details for organizing and conducting the simulation are set forth in the four documents which follow this introduction. In the following paragraphs, a brief set of descriptions will be provided to give an interested user an overview of the simulation. It is important to reemphasize that the basic structure and operation of the simulation can be directly applied to any trial for which a transcript is available for student use.

The May 4th civil trial simulation can be conducted with as few as 20 students and as many as 50 students. The specific roles are: four lawyers, two each for the plaintiffs and defendants; five defendants, three plaintiffs, and two witnesses, all of whom give testimony during the trial; and from six to 36 jurors. I have always served as the trial judge, complete with flowing black robe and gavel. A graduate student usually serves as bailiff. Students are allowed to select the roles they want, and their first choices are honored as far as possible. The flexibility in the number of participants obviously relates to the number and size of the juries. The simulation has been conducted with a minimum of one six-person jury and a maximum of three 12-person juries. When there is more than one jury, each jury gives an independent verdict.

While the length of time for the simulation can vary, the simulation requires a minimum of five hours, which also seems to be an optimal time allotment. This breaks down to approximately three hours for opening and closing statements and interrogation of each witness, one hour for jury deliberation, and an hour for evaluation of the simulation. I consider the five-hour allotment optimal, for any less time rushes the simulation, too much and more time probably results in the onset of diminishing returns, although students usually express the wish for a longer time period. The simulation can be run in a single five-hour period, or it can be conducted for one-hour periods throughout the week. I have not found one approach to be superior. If the simulation is required for the course, then I will schedule it for the regular class periods when the class meets. If the simulation is an optional activity for extra credit, then I schedule it for a Saturday morning or afternoon.

The physical facilities required are simple, and no computational facilities are required. Any room is satisfactory that can accommodate the number of students in the simulation. I have found, however, that the mood of the simulation is more somber when the trial is held in a room that has the appearance of a courtroom rather than a regular classroom. Among the possibilities for a physical setting would be a local courtroom. The one indispensable item for the simulation is a complete transcript of the trial. The Akron law firm of Blakemore, Rosen, and Norris donated a copy of the 1975 trial transcript to the Kent State University library.

Student preparation for the simulation varies substantially, depending upon the role which a student plays. By far the most demanding role is that of a lawyer. Student lawyers must do background research on the May 4th shootings, carefully read the testimonies of each witness, develop an overall strategy for the trial, and prepare a detailed set of questions for each witness. Because of this heavy workload, I offer two hours of individual research credit for each lawyer in the simulation. I have never had problems recruiting lawyers, for pre-law students are anxious to have this type of learning experience. Students in the roles of plaintiffs, defendants, and witnesses have some outside preparation, for they must read and prepare a written summary of the portion of the trial transcript pertaining to their testimony. This requires five to ten hours of work. Jurors' preparation involves the least amount of work, for they are only required to read the documents dealing with the opening instructions to the jury and the judge's charge to the jury.

A few words need to be said about my own preparation for the simulation. The creation of the simulation occupied a substantial portion of my research time during the quarter when it was developed, but now the simulation demands a modest amount of time. The primary time commitments currently involve periodic meetings with the lawyers and the actual conduct of the simulation if it is held on a weekend.

Student reaction to the simulation has been most favorable. Students invariably have rated the simulation as the best learning activity in the course, with most students rating the experience excellent on a five-point scale from excellent to poor. One needs to question, however, whether the student reaction is based more upon participation in a rather unique, intrinsically "fun" activity rather than upon the actual learning which occurs. I do not have a definitive answer to this question. To attempt to maximize the learning experience, it seems important to review the simulation activity with the students, emphasizing the extent to which the simulation paralleled and deviated from reality. I have found it especially valuable to include an essay question on the final examination, thus requiring students to reflect critically on the simulation experience.

INSTRUCTIONS FOR SIMULATION LAWYERS

I. *Overview.* The lawyers will be the primary actors in the civil trial simulation, and hence a great deal of responsibility rests upon each one of you. This sheet seeks to define the various activities which you must undertake to make the simulation a success. As you proceed, please keep in constant touch with me about developments; while it is impossible to anticipate all of the potential problems which may arise, we can be sure that some will indeed pop up. The one problem that can clearly be anticipated is that there will be a time crunch; consequently, you must begin to prepare immediately and to recognize that many hours of work lie ahead of you.

II. *Preparation for the Simulation.* Three basic sources need to be utilized. First of all, I suggest that you read the Scranton Commission's *The Kent State Tragedy*. Second, you should go to the Archives on the 11th floor of the library and ask for the 1975 clippings of the *Akron Beacon Journal* dealing with May 4th related events. These clippings will overview the trial for you and suggest directions in regard to the strategy you want to follow. It is at this point that each team of lawyers will want to develop its overall strategy and make divisions of labor. The third source you will have to use is the microfilm of the 1975 trial transcript, which contains the testimony of each witness as well as the opening and closing statements. The *Index to the Microfilm Copy of the May 4 Civil Trial Transcript* is on reserve at the library; it is filed under *Stegh, Les,* who compiled the index. The index will tell you who said what to whom when, and it will identify the reel which you need to ask for downstairs in the Microfilm Department.

You will need to specify exactly the reel which you want (the reel number). The Microfilm Center's hours are:

Monday-Thursday: 7:30 a.m.-9:45 p.m.
Friday: 6:00 a.m.-4:45 p.m.
Saturday: 9:00 a.m.-5:45 p.m.
Sunday: 1:00 p.m.-9:45 p.m.

III. *Paper.* Lawyers enrolling for two hours of research will be required to write a paper in which you analyze the legal issues and strategies which you used in the simulation. I would like for you to draw upon your readings and lectures from the judicial process class in preparing the paper. The paper can be jointly written if you wish. The outline for the paper might take the following form:

1. Introduction: Purpose and Organization
2. Description of Legal Issues and Verdict Sought
3. Description of Strategies
   A. Pre-trial discussions and planning
   B. Opening statements
   C. Witness interrogation
   D. Closing statements
4. Analysis of the Simulation

IV. *Grading.* Your grade will be based equally upon (1) preparation for and participation in the simulation, and (2) the paper.

V. *Additional Documents.* There will be three additional handouts which you will want to examine closely: (1) "1978 Krause v. Rhodes Simulation," which is a general guide for all members of the simulation, (2) "Judge Hensley's Opening Instructions to Jurors," and (3) "Judge Hensley's Charge to the Jury."

1978 KRAUSE v. RHODES SIMULATION

Nature and Purposes. During the past decade, an exciting development has occurred in the teaching of the social sciences. This development, known as simulation, has been an important innovation in classroom instruction. Involving students as participants in operating models of social situations, a simulation attempts to replicate in the class a set of events which might happen in the real world.

Our simulation focuses upon the current federal civil litigation which has arisen from the May 4th, 1970 shootings at Kent State University. A 1975 federal district court resulted in a 9-3 jury verdict that none of the defendants was liable for damages stemming from the shootings. This decision was appealed before the Sixth Circuit Court of Appeals, where lawyers for the plaintiffs sought either a new trial or a reversal of the lower court's decision. The appeals court ruled in favor of the plaintiffs, ordering a new trial to be held because of the judge's improper handling of a threat to one of the jurors. Drawing upon the transcript from the 1975 trial, we will therefore be conducting a simulation of the upcoming federal district court case of Krause v. Rhodes to determine if any of the defendants can be held liable for damages in connection with the May 4, 1970 shootings.

While the simulation will hopefully be similar in many important ways to the upcoming trial, it is important to recognize that we have to make many simplifications. Two are especially critical to note. First, the actual trial will involve as many as nine guard officers and 17 guard members as defendants. In our simulation, we have only two guard officers and two guard enlisted men in order to simplify and shorten our simulation. Second, while the actual trial will involve several major legal issues, our simulation will focus on one issue: did the defendants knowingly subject the plaintiffs to a denial of their constitutional right not to be deprived of life or liberty without due process of law?

It is hoped that a number of learning objectives can be achieved through the simulation exercise. Most fundamentally, we are attempting to provide students with a learning experience supplemental to the more traditional methods of classroom instruction. From this simulation it is anticipated that students can acquire valuable insights into (1) the events surrounding the May 4th shootings, (2) the legal issues associated with the civil trial, and (3) the processes of the American judicial system. In addition to serving as a valuable learning experience, it is also hoped that the simulation will serve to increase students' interests in these events and processes, thereby stimulating further study and research.

While the advantages of simulation exercises are numerous, a word of caution is also necessary. The success of this exercise depends solely upon the willingness of students to become active participants. In most games, if players do not perform the roles as set forth, then the game is of little fun. Similarly, in simulation if someone doesn't follow the rules or carry out the assigned role, then the experience for all students is put in jeopardy. Consequently, each participant must assume his or her role seriously, and must be diligent in preparation for the simulation and consistent in carrying out the assigned role. Failure to do this may endanger the learning experience for the entire class.

Perhaps the central word of the preceeding paragraph is that of preparation. To achieve proper preparation, each student must review the guidelines in this handout, most carefully research the position of the person being represented in the simulation, and should consult with other relevant members in the simulation. If this type of careful preparation is done, all of us will find the simulation to be an enjoyable, stimulating, and effective learning experience.

Preparation for the Simulation: Defendants, Plaintiffs, Witnesses. In addition to attending class each day, there are several basic sources which can be used in preparing for the simulation. One is the Scranton Commission's *The Kent State Tragedy,* which will give you a general overview of the 1970 events. Also useful in providing a general overview is Jim Best's "Kent State: Answers and Questions" in Hensley and Lewis, eds., *Kent State and May 4th: A Social Science Perspective.* Another source which is useful in gaining an overview of the legal process which has stemmed from the shootings is Tom Hensley's "The Kent State Trials" in Hensley and Lewis' *Kent State and May 4th.* A more detailed summary of the 1975 trial can be found in the *Akron Beacon Journal* newspaper clippings in the Archives of the library, located on the 11th floor. All of the above sources are recommended but not required. The final source, the microfilm copy of the May 4th civil trial transcript, *must* be utilized. The *Index to the Microfilm Copy of the May 4 Civil Trial Transcript* is on reserve at the library. It is filed under Steigh, Les, who compiled the index. The *Index* will tell you who said what to whom, and it will identify the reel which you need to ask for downstairs (basement) in the Microfilm Department.

Each student in the role of a defendant, plaintiff, or witness must prepare by November 17 a written summary of the position taken by the respective actor in the 1975 trial. This should be at least one typewritten page and is due in the judge's chambers no later than noon on the 17th. These documents will be reviewed by Judge Hensley and will be available to all lawyers.

Preparation for the Simulation: Jurors. Preparation by the jurors takes a very different form than does preparation by the other simulation participants. Instead of studying portions of the 1975 transcript, jurors must study *carefully* two documents which will be handed out one week prior to the simulation. These documents are entitled "Judge Hensley's Opening Instructions to the Jury" and "Judge Hensley's Charge to the Jury." The documents specify the procedures which will govern the trial and the precise legal questions involved in the case. *Careful study* of these documents by each juror *prior* to the simulation is imperative in order for each jury to reach a fair and speedy decision.

JUDGE HENSLEY'S OPENING INSTRUCTIONS TO JURORS

Good afternoon, ladies and gentlemen of the jury. As this trial begins, it is my duty to instruct you briefly as to the rules and procedures which must guide your actions and thoughts throughout this most historic trial. I will try not to take long, but several very important points must be made.

You have been selected because of the standards of objectivity and fairness which you have professed; and you have each taken an oath to set aside all previous opinions concerning the events surrounding the shootings at Kent State University on May 4th, 1970, and to make your judgments in this case solely upon the evidence introduced at this trial. The very foundation of the American judicial system is based upon individuals' ability to function as impartial jurors, and the challenge to you in such an emotional case as this one is indeed great. I have the utmost confidence in each and every one of you, however, and I know that you shall not disappoint me.

Throughout this trial, you may be subjected to a variety of pressures, both subtle and direct. We may find members of the press covering the trial, and your friends will likely become aware of your jury activities. Through these and other avenues, you may find attempts being made to influence your decisions. You must avoid any such attempts insofar as you can, and you must not allow these efforts—should they be made—to influence you in any way. Do not discuss the trial with anyone at any time, and remember that your votes will never be known to anyone outside the jury room.

There are certain rules which apply to the trial of all civil actions, including this one. These should be explained to and understood by you, in order that you can correctly decide the particular problems, or issues, as they are called, involved in this litigation. *The burden is on the plaintiffs in a civil action such as this, to prove every essential element of plaintiffs' claims by a preponderance of the evidence. If the proof should fail to establish any essential element of plaintiffs' claims by a preponderance of the evidence in this case, the jury should find for the defendants.* To "establish a preponderance of the evidence" means to prove that something is more likely so than not so. In other words, a preponderance of the evidence in the case means such evidence as, when considered and compared with that opposed to it, has more convincing force, and produces in your minds belief that what is sought to be proved is more likely true than not true.

In considering whether any fact in issue has been proved by a preponderance of the evidence in the case, the jury may consider the testimony of all witnesses, regardless of who may have called them, and all exhibits received in evidence, regardless of who may have produced them.

It is the quality of the evidence that must be weighed, and quality may or may not be identical with quantity.

There are, generally speaking, two types of evidence from which a jury may properly find the truth as to the facts of a case. One is direct evidence—such as the testimony of an eyewitness. The other is indirect or circumstantial evidence—the proof of a chain of circumstances pointing to the existence or non-existence of certain facts.

As a general rule, the law makes no distinction between direct and circumstantial evidence, but simply requires that the jury find the facts in accordance with the preponderance of all the evidence in the case, both direct and circumstantial.

Statements and arguments of counsel are not evidence in this case, unless made as an admission of fact or stipulation of fact. When the attorneys on both sides stipulate or agree as to the existence of a fact, the jury must accept the stipulation as evidence and regard the fact as conclusively proved.

The test is not which side brings the greater number of witnesses, or presents the greater quantity of evidence; but which witness, and which evidence, appeals to your minds as being most accurate, and otherwise trustworthy. You, as jurors, are the sole judges of the credibility of the witnesses and the weight their testimony deserves.

The evidence in the case always consists of the sworn testimony of the witnesses, regardless of who may have called them; and all exhibits received in evidence, regardless of who may have produced them; and all applicable presumptions stated in these instructions.

Any evidence as to which an objection was sustained by the Court, and any evidence ordered stricken by the Court, must be strictly disregarded.

Anything you may have seen or heard outside the courtroom touching the merits of the case is not evidence, and must be entirely disregarded.

You are to consider only the evidence in the case, but in your consideration you are not limited to the bald statements of the witnesses. In other words, you are not limited solely to what you see and hear as the witnesses testify. On the contrary, you are permitted to draw, from facts which you find have been proved, such reasonable inferences as seem justified in the light of your experience.

You are not bound to decide any issue of fact in accordance with the testimony of any number of witnesses, which does not produce in your minds belief in the likelihood of truth, as against the testimony of a lesser number of witnesses, or other evidence, which does not produce such belief in your minds.

The rules of evidence ordinarily do not permit witnesses to testify as to opinions or conclusions. An exception to this rule exists as to those whom we call "expert witnesses." Witnesses who, by education and experience, have become expert in some art, science, profession, or calling, may state an opinion as to relevant material matter, in which they profess to be expert, and may also state their reasons for the opinion.

However, if you should decide that the opinion of an expert witness is not based upon sufficient education and experience, or if you should conclude that the reasons given in support of the opinion are not sound, you may reject the opinion entirely.

In the present action certain testimony has the potential to be introduced by way of deposition. You are instructed that this testimony is entitled to the same consideration, the same rebuttable presumption that the witness speaks the truth, and the same judgment on your part with reference to its weight, as the testimony of witnesses who have confronted you on the witness stand, and you are not to discount it merely because it comes to you in the form of a deposition.

This concludes my opening instructions to you. Listen carefully, think clearly, and decide objectively. No one can ask you to do any more than this, but you are under a most serious obligation to do no less.

JUDGE HENSLEY'S CHARGE TO THE JURY

Ladies and gentlemen, it is my duty to charge you as to the law in this case. While you are sole judges of the facts and credibility of the witnesses, your oath requires that you accept the law as it is given by the Court, and to apply that law in your deliberations. You are not permitted to change the law, nor to apply your own conception of what you think the law should be.

These cases, which have been tried together, involve claims of damages for injuries and deaths suffered by various plaintiffs shortly after noon on May 4, 1970, upon the campus of Kent State University. The defendants deny the allegations of the plaintiffs and also allege affirmatively that they were justified in acting as they did at the time and place in question, and that the plaintiffs' injuries were the result of their own conduct.

The burden is on the plaintiffs in a civil action such as this, to prove every essential element of plaintiffs' claims by a preponderance of the evidence. If the proof should fail to establish any essential element of plaintiffs' claims by a preponderance of the evidence in the case, the jury should find for the defendants. To "establish a preponderance of the evidence" means to prove that something is more likely so than not so. The test is not which side brings the greater number of witnesses, or presents the greater quantity of evidence; but which witness, and which evidence, appeals to your minds as being most accurate, and otherwise trustworthy. You, as jurors, are the sole judges of the credibility of the witnesses and the weight their testimony deserves.

Although this case has been tried as if it were one lawsuit, actually it involves a large number of different actions among the various parties. There are 13 separate plaintiffs or groups of plaintiffs as follows:

Arthur Krause, father of Allison Krause
Elaine Miller, mother of Jeffrey Miller
Sarah Scheuer, mother of Sandy Scheuer
Louis Schroeder, father of William Schroeder
John Cleary
Donald Scott MacKenzie
Douglas Wrentmore
Thomas Grace
James Russell
Alan Canfora
Dean Kahler
Joseph Lewis
Robert Stamps

Each of the 13 plaintiffs is making claims against five different defendants:

James Rhodes, Governor of Ohio; Sylvester Del Corso, Adjutant General of the Ohio National Guard at the time and place in question; Robert Canterbury, officer of the Ohio National Guard at the time and place in question; and Lawrence Shafer and Myron Pryor, members of the Ohio National Guard at the time and place in question.

We now turn to the specific rules under which plaintiffs are bringing suit. Plaintiffs allege the defendants named above knowingly subjected the plaintiffs to the deprivation of the following right and privilege secured and protected to them by the Constitution and laws of the United States, namely:

The right not to be deprived of life or liberty without due process of law:

The statutory authority for these claims is Section 1983 of Title 42 of the United States Code Annotated, which provides that any inhabitant of this Federal District may seek redress in this Court by way of damages, against any person or persons who, under color of any law, statute, ordinance, regulation, or custom, knowingly subject such inhabitant to the deprivation of any rights, privileges, or immunities, secured or protected by the Constitution or laws of the United States.

The defendants deny any violations of constitutional rights and allege that all of their acts and conducts of which plaintiffs complain were done in pursuance of defendants' lawful authority, and lawful duty, as officers of the state of Ohio, to protect the persons and property of the citizens of said state, from injury or damage as the result of violent or tumultuous conduct of a large number of people, which created a clear and present danger to the safety of persons and property, and generally to enforce the laws of the state of Ohio.

In any claim of a violation of the right not to be deprived of life or liberty without due process of law, the burden is upon the plaintiffs by a preponderance of the evidence in the case that these rights were violated. The 14th Amendment guarantee that no state shall "deprive any person of life, liberty, or property without due process of law" is not absolute or unqualified. It is always subject to reasonable restraints, including, of course, such restraints as are imposed by law. Further, unless the evidence in the case leads the jury to a different or contrary conclusion, the presumption is that the law has been obeyed.

One element of liberty is that of being free from unlawful attacks upon the physical integrity of one's person. It has always been the policy of the law to protect the physical integrity of every person from unauthorized violation or interference.

To be deprived of life or liberty "without due process of law" means to be deprived of life or liberty without authority of law. Before the jury can determine, then, whether or not any of the plaintiffs were deprived by any of the defendants of any of their liberties under the Federal Constitution, or any of their lives "without due process of law," the jury must first determine, from a preponderance of evidence in the case, whether the defendants, or any of them, acted within or without the bounds of their lawful authority under State law. As to this matter, it must be borne in mind that there are very considerable differences in authority under State law among the various defendants, some of them having much greater authority than others. If the defendants, or any of them, acted within the limits of their lawful authority under State law as to any of the plaintiffs, then such defendant or defendants could not have deprived any such plaintiff of any liberty, or of life, "without due process of law."

Due process of law means, among other things, that no one can be punished until he has been convicted and sentenced by a court with authority to act in his case. In other words, public officials charged with the duty of enforcing the laws do not have the authority to punish a person in the process of preventing that person from, or apprehending that person for, the commission of a violation of law, even though they observe that person violating, or about to violate, the law. Punishment can only be lawful if it is based on the sentence of a court following a judgment of guilty.

At this point, I should point out to you a point that has been made in other contexts: at the present state of this trial, you will not be concerned with any amount of damages but rather will limit your considerations to whether plaintiffs are entitled to recover any damages at all.

The issues which you are to determine in this case will now be outlined to you. Although it may be somewhat repetitive to do so, this will be done separately as to each of the separate defendants that were listed near the beginning of the instructions.

I. Issues as to the Defendant James A. Rhodes

FIRST, (a) was the determination of the defendant Rhodes that it was necessary to call the Ohio National Guard to the city of Kent, including the campus of Kent State University, a reasonable judgment made in good faith after a proper investigation of the circumstances then and there existing; (b) or did this defendant act outside the scope of his lawful authority, abuse his discretion or fail to act in good faith in formulating or promulgating or delegating to subordinates the authority to formulate or promulgate standards and regulations for the training and actions of the Ohio National Guard in the handling of riots or civil disturbances to such an extent that such standards and regulations were materially different from these prescribed by the Department of Army of the United States or those in use generally throughout the United States and either required or made inevitable the use of fatal force in suppressing civil disorders when the circumstances at the critical time were such that non-lethal force would suffice to restore order and the use of lethal force was unnecessary?

If your answer to part (a) is "yes" and to part (b) is "no," then you need go no further, but should return a verdict in favor of the defendant James A. Rhodes; but if your answer to part (a) is "no," or to part (b) is "yes," then you have a second issue, namely:

SECOND, did any of the plaintiffs or plaintiffs' decedents suffer any deprivation of any constitutional right or liberty without due process of law, as that phrase is explained in these instructions, by reason of this defendant's alleged acts or conduct?

If your answer to this second question is "no," then you should return a verdict in favor of the defendant James A. Rhodes; but if your answer to this second question is "yes," then you should return a verdict in favor of the plaintiffs.

II. Issues as to the Defendant Sylvester Del Corso

FIRST, did the defendant Sylvester Del Corso (a) fail properly to determine and advise the Governor concerning the necessity to dispatch the Ohio National Guard to the city of Kent, including the campus of Kent State University; or (b) did this defendant have the responsibility for formulating and promulgating the standards and regulations of training and conduct of the Ohio National Guard for handling riots and civil disturbances, and if so, did he abuse his discretion or fail to act in good faith in formulating and promulgating such standards and regulations, to such an extent that such standards and regulations were materially different from those prescribed by the Department of Army of the United States or those in use generally throughout the United States and either required or made inevitable the use of fatal force in suppressing civil disorders when the circumstances at the critical time were such that non-lethal force would suffice to restore order and the use of lethal force was unnecessary?

If your answer to all these questions is "no," you need go no further, but should return a verdict in favor of the defendant Sylvester Del Corso; but if your answer to any of them is "yes," then you have a second issue to determine, namely:

SECOND, did any of the plaintiffs or plaintiffs' decedents suffer the deprivation of any constitutional right without due process of law, as that term is explained in these instructions, by reason of the alleged acts and conduct of the defendant?

If your answer to this question is "no," then you should return a verdict in favor of the defendant Sylvester Del Corso; but if your answer to this second question is "yes," then you should return a verdict in favor of the plaintiffs.

III. Issues as to the Defendant Robert H. Canterbury

FIRST, (a) were the decisions made, the actions taken or the orders given by the defendant while on duty in the city of Kent or on the campus of Kent State University reasonable and made in good faith after proper investigation and with full understanding of all the circumstances then and there existing; (b) did the defendants use, order the use of, or aid, abet and encourage the use of, fatal force in suppressing a civil disorder at the time and place stated when the circumstances at that critical time were such that non-lethal force would suffice in order to restore order and the use of lethal force was unnecessary?

If your answer to part (a) of these questions is "yes" and to part (b) is "no," then you need go no further, but should return a verdict in favor of the defendant; but if your answer to part (a) is "no," or to part (b) is "yes," then you have a second issue to determine, namely:

SECOND, did any of the plaintiffs or plaintiffs' decedents suffer any deprivation of any constitutional right or liberty without due process of law, as that phrase is explained in these instructions, by reason of the alleged acts or conduct of the defendant?

If your answer to this second question is "no," then you should return a verdict in favor of the defendant; but if your answer to this second question is "yes," then you should return a verdict in favor of the plaintiffs.

IV. Issues as to the Defendants Lawrence Shafer and Myron Pryor

FIRST, (a) were the decisions made and the actions taken by these defendants on the campus of Kent State University on Monday, May 4, 1970, reasonable and made in good faith with full understanding of all of the circumstances then and there existing; or (b) did any or all of these defendants knowingly use force, while acting under color of state law, or the standards and regulations of the Ohio National Guard, outside the bounds of his lawful authority under state law or the standards and regulations of the Ohio National Guard; or (c) did either of these defendants use, order the use of, or aid, abet and encourage the use, fatal force in suppressing a civil disorder at the time and place stated when the circumstances at that critical time were such that non-lethal force would suffice in order to restore order and the use of lethal force was unnecessary?

If your answer to part (a) of these questions is "yes" and to parts (b) and (c) is "no," then you need go no further, but should return a verdict or verdicts in favor of such defendant or defendants; but if your answer to part (a) is "no," or to either part (b) or (c) is "yes," as to any one or more of the defendants, then as to any such defendant or defendants you have a second issue to determine, namely:

SECOND, did any of the plaintiffs or plaintiffs' decedents suffer any deprivation of any constitutional right or liberty without due process of law, as that phrase is explained in these instructions, by reason of the alleged acts or conduct of any one or more of these defendants.

If your answer to this second question is "no" as to any one or more or all of these defendants, then you should return a verdict in favor of such defendant or defendants; but if your answer to this second question is "yes," then you should return a verdict in favor of the plaintiffs.

Let me now begin to conclude my instructions to you. This is a case that appeals to one's sympathies, but sympathy has no place in the trial of a lawsuit, and in making up your minds as to what your verdict shall be, do not permit your deliberations on the evidence to be influenced by the slightest degree by the result or effect of your verdict.

It is your duty, as jurors, to consult with one another, and to deliberate with a view to reaching an agreement, if you can do so without violence to individual judgment. Each of you must decide the case for yourself, but do so only after impartial consideration of the evidence in the case with your fellow jurors. In the course of your deliberations, do not hesitate to reexamine your own views, and change your opinion, if convinced it is erroneous. But do not surrender your honest conviction as to the weight or effect of evidence, solely because of the opinion of your fellow jurors, or for the mere purpose of returning a verdict.

Remember at all times, you are not partisans. You are judges—judges of the facts. Your sole interest is to ascertain the truth from the evidence in the case.

By stipulation and agreement of the parties in this case you may reach a verdict upon the concurrence of three-fourths or more of your number. Whenever three-fourths of the members of the jury have reached a verdict in each case, you may conclude your deliberations and those concurring in the verdict should sign it on the spaces provided for your signature.

It is not necessary for the foreperson to sign the verdict if he or she is not among your number who concur in it.

As you have been previously instructed, there are 13 separate cases before you. Thus you will be given 13 separate forms of verdict, one for each case, upon which you can return all possible verdicts in that particular case. For your convenience, the verdict forms have been drafted in such a way that you can complete each one by simply placing "X" marks in the appropriate boxes to express your conclusions. Omitting the formal caption, the verdict forms read as follows:

It starts out with a pair of brackets, and following that it says:

"We, the jury, on the issues joined, find in favor of the plaintiff Arthur Krause, Administrator and against all defendants jointly and severally."

Then, again, there is a set of brackets for you to mark in, if you desire:

"We, the jury, on the issues joined find in favor of all the defendants against the plaintiff, Arthur Krause, Administrator."

Then if neither of those two alternatives are used, the form goes on to say:

"We, the jury, on the issue joined, in the case of Arthur Krause, Administrator, with respect to each of the defendants find as follows."

Then there are three caption headings, one heading, "Defendant," and the second caption heading, "In favor of the plaintiff." Third caption heading, "In favor of the defendant."

Under the caption heading, "Defendant," there are the names of each of the defendants in the case. Opposite each name, under the heading, "In favor of the plaintiff," there is a pair of brackets making a space in which you can indicate a verdict. And there is a similar bracket under the caption heading, "In favor of the defendant," so that you can be selective by marking in favor of the plaintiffs as to some of the defendants and in favor of the defendants as to others.

Then at the bottom of the form there are signature lines, the last of which has marked "Foreman" or "Forelady." As I have explained to you, as soon as three-fourths of you have concurred in any particular verdict, you can find that form. If the foreman or forelady doesn't concur in the verdict, naturally he or she won't sign it, the fact that there is a specific blank for his or her signature doesn't make any difference.

After you have completed each of the verdict forms, all those jurors concurring in the verdict, but not less than three-fourths should sign each verdict form. You cannot return a verdict in any of these cases unless three-fourths or more of your number concur in it.

When you retire to the jury room, you will be in the charge of the court bailiff, and he will in turn notify the Court.

KRAUSE V. RHODES (1977)

VERDICT FORM CONCERNING PLAINTIFF _____

[   ] We, the jury, on the issues, joined, find in favor of the plaintiff _____
_____ and against all defendants jointly and severally.

[   ] We, the jury, on the issues joined, find in favor of all the defendants against the plaintiff, _____.

We, the jury, on the issues joined, in the case of _____
_____ with respect to each of the defendants find as follows:

Defendant	In Favor of the Plaintiff	In Favor of the Defendant
James A. Rhodes	[ ]	[ ]
Sylvester Del Corso	[ ]	[ ]
Robert Canterbury	[ ]	[ ]
Lawrence Shafer	[ ]	[ ]
Myron Pryor	[ ]	[ ]

Signatures:

_____   _____

_____   _____

_____   _____

_____   _____

_____   _____

Foreman or Forelady

Frogtown:
A Simulation of Urban Politics

William C. Johnson
Bethel College

This game was developed to give students experience in role-playing and decision-making for an actual urban community. Its beginning point approximates the current status of that community, and the objective is to plan its future. The decision-making processes of the game also resemble, within the limits imposed by the learning conditions, the ones that will actually be used in that city. Thus students gain an element of realism by being able to view the community and relate it to its political and geographical context.

"Frogtown" is the nickname of an old working-class neighborhood in central St. Paul that was entering upon a period of renewal when the game was first devised in 1972. Actually, only the eastern half of the neighborhood is under consideration here, so the class materials make reference to "East Frogtown." Any community can be used, but one that is on the verge of major change offers the most realism. It should also be one that faces several different options for its future development, so that no single outcome is certain and the choices will generate significant political debate.

Frogtown was used in an introductory course in urban politics, and most students had no previous courses in college political science. It was played near the end of the term so as to utilize all the course materials, especially the unit on housing and urban renewal. No additional preparation was required of the students. However, it is important that students have seen the neighborhood and grasped the fact that they will deal with real people and structures.

As presented here, the game works best with 15-25 students, allowing for one Chairperson and two or three on each role position. There are nine roles on the East Frogtown Planning Committee, although seven or eight would be workable. No special facilities are needed, although some additional space for group caucuses should be obtained if the classroom is small. A large wall map of the neighborhood should be available so that alternatives can be explained to the whole class easily.

The game has been played in separate 50- or 60-minute class periods. On the first day, the descriptive materials were distributed and students chose their roles. This allowed them a day or two to think ahead and meet with their fellow role-players if they wished. The game opened as the members stated their initial positions, whether in support of a plan given to them, a plan of their own devising, or some general features of an acceptable plan. After that, the bargaining began in an effort to formulate a composite plan that the necessary majority could accept. Agreement of any five members validated the plan and ended the game. Experience showed that three class periods normally sufficed to reach a conclusion. On the following class day, a debriefing session was held to confirm what was learned, evaluate the experience, and consider possible improvements. Students were graded on attendance and activity.

The materials given the students included the following:

(1) a street map of the neighborhood, indicating the major landmarks, uses of land, and general condition of structures;

(2) a verbal description of the neighborhood, stressing the kinds of information that planners normally use;

(3) a description of five alternative plans for the neighborhood that had already been laid before the committee, each formulated by one of the groups represented on the East Frogtown Planning Committee;

(4) a set of limiting conditions to keep the bargaining within some bounds of realism (note: this is the hardest part of the game to manage effectively);

(5) the roles on the East Frogtown Planning Committee, which is to recommend a renewal program to the mayor of St. Paul.

EAST FROGTOWN: A Blue-Collar Neighborhood in Transition

Area: About 40 city blocks, enclosed by Como, Rice, University and Western Avenues.

Population: About 4,000.

Origin: Settled in the period 1870-1900 by German, Austrian, Polish, Hungarian, and Irish immigrants, who worked in the nearby factories and railroad yards.

Social Characteristics: The people are slightly older than the city average, although there are many children. Their average income is slightly lower than the average. It is fairly stable, as many have deep roots in the neighborhood and take pride in it. A fairly large percentage own their homes. Nearly all of them are white. Most are Catholic.

Physical Conditions: East Frogtown has a mixture of houses, some well-kept, but many run-down and dilapidated. A few have been bought by the city Housing and Redevelopment Authority for demolition and replacement. The lots are narrow, some as little as 20 feet wide. Vacant lots are few (most of them the result of demolition), and the houses are close together and close to the street. Most houses hold one or two families, and some lots have two houses, front and back. The streets are narrow, and lack curbs in some blocks. Marion Street carries heavy through traffic. There is good bus service along Rice, Thomas, and University. There is a new recreation center along Como, between Galtier and Marion, with a playground.

Business and Institutions: The neighborhood's main business district is on Rice

Street, with a few stores on University, Western, and scattered elsewhere. Some stores are rundown, while many others are well-kept. Most of them serve the immediate neighborhood with food, hardware, etc. St. Adalbert's Catholic Church and school at Charles and Galtier has historically served the Polish community, while St. Vincent's at Blair and Virginia is regarded as the "Irish" Catholic Church. The closest public school is on Edmund, one block west of Western. The former parochial school next to St. Vincent's is now the "Little Red Schoolhouse," operated by the American Indian Movement. There is an old factory at Como and Galtier, that makes printing equipment.

Surroundings: North of Como Avenue is industrial and commercial property. East of Rice Street there is one block of old residences, then the large Bethesda Lutheran Hospital. Southeast of Rice and University is the State Capitol complex, and beyond that, downtown St. Paul. Sears Roebuck has a large store one block south of University, between Marion and Rice. To the west of Sears is a public housing project with a large black population. West of Western Avenue is the rest of the Frogtown area, but with better quality housing for the most part. A large ice arena is on Minnehaha west of Western. In summary, the neighborhood is surrounded by good shopping facilities and means of transportation. It is at the heart of St. Paul, virtually the crossroads of the city. There are many jobs within easy commuting distance, excellent medical and cultural facilities, and a variety of means of entertainment.

ALTERNATIVES FOR EAST FROGTOWN

The very characteristics of East Frogtown just described make it a focal point for city-wide interest. Obviously, its future development could be in any of several very different directions, and many groups are interested in seeing it develop according to their values. So, two questions are crucial: What kind of neighborhood should East Frogtown be in future years? Who shall decide it? Five development plans have already been put forth, and others that are modifications and compromises among these are also possible. Here are the basic five:

Plan A: Capitol West New Town. Calls for total clearance and rebuilding of entire areas over a 10-20-year time span, beginning with the eastern section and moving west. There will be large commercial office buildings along Rice and University, with a hotel complex at the intersection of those two streets. Marion Street will become a shopping center, with all car traffic on a lower-level street, and a pedestrian mall above it. A large parking ramp between Marion and Rice will serve customers and employees. The remainder of the area will be filled in with high-rise apartments, townhouses, and garden apartments for middle-to-upper income persons. Significant open space will be left for recreation. A people-mover transit system will connect this area with the capitol area and

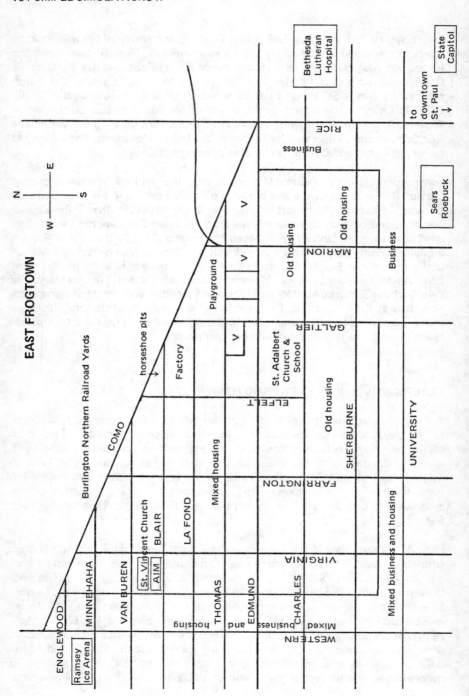

EAST FROGTOWN

downtown St. Paul. Since most of this development will be privately financed and owned, it will provide important tax revenues to the city. Most important, it will be a high-density use of land appropriate to such a central-city location.

Plan B: The People's Plan. Calls for large-scale clearance of area, but exempting the homes in better condition in the western portion. In the cleared area, there will be low-rise apartments and townhouses, constructed with government assistance, for low-to-middle income groups. A new shopping center at Rice and University will provide locations for small businessmen, especially those of minority groups, with government aid to help new ones get started. Along University, west of Rice, there will be a new public school complex to provide compensatory education for the disadvantaged and meet a number of special education needs which the St. Paul schools are not now fulfilling. In the center of the area, there will be a park and community center where various groups can meet for social, cultural, and recreational purposes. It would also include a day care center and nursery school for children of working mothers.

Plan C: Frogdale. Envisions the upgrading of business establishments along Rice and University Avenues and for new commercial construction on vacant lots east of Marion and south of Sherburne to expand business opportunities and draw more customers from all over the city. There will be the hotel complex also planned for Capitol West. At Rice and Como there will be a large arcade in which small businessmen could rent space at low cost. In the first blocks to the west of Marion and north of Sherburne there will be some high-density housing to replace the deteriorated structures and provide more steady customers but the remainder of the area would not be touched by this plan.

Plan D: Seniortown. Will clear the old housing areas in the east and south sections and rebuild them with high-rise and garden apartments exclusively or largely for the elderly. Somewhere in the center there will be a large medical clinic and senior citizens center to meet the social, physical, and recreational needs of the elderly throughout the city. This senior citizen area would likely expand into the rest of East Frogtown gradually, as the funds become available, but care would be taken not to displace elderly persons if their present homes are in good condition.

Plan E: F.R.O.G. (Frogtown Residents On Guard). Plans no mass demolition, but rather the preservation of the residential character of the community and no expansion of commercial facilities. Deteriorated houses will be replaced with good-quality single- or two-family dwellings, and current residents will receive government loans or grants to upgrade homes that are still in good condition. The city will expand park and playground facilities and improve streets and sidewalks. Some streets will be closed to access from Como, Rice, and University to reduce traffic and noise.

Limiting Conditions: For the purpose of this game, assume that the amount of financial aid that can be expected from the federal and state governments over the next five years is only enough to do *one* of the following:

(1) buy and clear *half* of the land in East Frogtown,

(2) construct residences for 2,000 persons,

(3) build any two of the following: business arcade, senior citizen medical-social center, compensatory education school, general community center,

(4) recondition and upgrade *half* of the residences in East Frogtown (part of these may be combined in appropriate proportions).

Funds for other projects must come from either the city (whose resources are very limited), the private money market (which could be a source of substantial amounts, but only for projects that are economically sound and self-supporting), or possibly a private foundation (these like to support projects that are innovative and imaginative as well as financially sound). This private support will be sufficient to (1) construct residences for 500 persons *or* (2) build the business arcade (but not both).

EAST FROGTOWN PLANNING COMMITTEE

This group has been appointed by Mayor Latimer to produce a coherent plan for the future of the neighborhood. As you can see, its members have distinct constituencies to represent or interests to protect, and they should try to do so as far as they are able. The agreement of *any five* of the nine members will validate the final plan. Thus, each member realizes that it is in his/her interest to take part in the bargaining in order to see that as much as possible of the original desires are integrated into that plan. Note that none of the original five plans is acceptable to a majority of the committee as it was presented, and so compromise is necessary. The basic object of this "game," then, is to be one of the "deciding five" while compromising as little as necessary of one's interests.

The committee members are:

1. Chairperson of the Greater Saint Paul Committee, which originated the CAPITOL WEST NEW TOWN plan. This group is made up of bankers, real estate interests, downtown businessmen, construction companies, and other civic notables. They want East Frogtown to be redeveloped to benefit the whole city, arguing that a site so close to downtown and the Capitol must be devoted to economically "higher" purposes than at present. The Chairperson is an affluent public relations executive who lives in the Highland Park area. He/she is strongly attracted to the "new town" concept and wants to demonstrate that St. Paul can make it work more successfully than Minneapolis has, and with private financing.

2. Action Coordinator of the Peoples Caucus. This is an organization made up of blacks, chicanos, native Americans, and liberal whites, which has sought better opportunities for housing, employment, education, and business prospects for minorities. It has two wings, one more militant than the other, and the

caucus always seems to be on the verge of breaking up. This Action Coordinator is a black social worker who lives just south of University Avenue from East Frogtown. This group originated the People's Plan. He/she might compromise with Plans C or D if enough concessions were made, but knows that the more militant wing would revolt if too much of the plan were given away. They strongly oppose both plans A and E, seeing both as efforts to keep minorities out of East Frogtown.

3. Director of the St. Paul chapter, American Indian Movement. AIM generally supports the Peoples Plan, but insists that a special area be reserved for a Native American school and cultural center, and that certain housing around that center be assigned exclusively for Indians, which the rest of the People's Caucus is reluctant to do in order to avoid the very kind of discrimination they denounce. As a result, AIM is open to discuss these demands with the proponents of other plans, especially C and D.

4. President of the Rice-University Merchants' Association. This organization of small merchants seeks to bring in more stores, provide better parking, and in general revitalize what has become a rather seedy business district. It originated Plan C to do these things, and is in a good position to get credit from major St. Paul banks for the project. While many of the merchants live elsewhere in the city or suburbs, the president owns a home in the neighborhood, at Thomas and Virginia. He/she is strongly opposed to plans A and B for both personal and business reasons, but would consider plans D or E if they were modified to provide for more business development.

5. Representative of the St. Paul Senior Citizens Association and Editor of *Gray Power,* a weekly newspaper distributed to all the senior citizens in the city. The organization works to secure more housing for the elderly and better medical and social services for them and has strong support from the oldsters of East Frogtown. There is a long waiting list of aged persons for the city's low-rent apartments. This representative is a retired 67-year-old advertising writer who owns a home just west of Frogtown but would like to sell it and move into a modern apartment, preferably in East Frogtown where many of his/her friends live. The organization spearheaded plan D, but could compromise with C. He/she would also consider Plan A if a significant part of the area were reserved for the elderly, including those with low incomes, and also Plan E if most of the new construction consisted of apartments for the elderly. But this largely white organization is very suspicious of Plan B.

6. Director of the Community Relations Office of the St. Paul Labor Council (AFL-CIO). The Council has no specific redevelopment plan of its own, but is primarily concerned to create more jobs for union members, and the more new construction takes place in East Frogtown, the better. From this perspective, plans A and B are best. But this person also realizes that many Frogtown residents are also union members, and their loyalty to their neighborhood usually come ahead of support for the unions. He/she is not a resident of the area, but has friends there and attends St. Vincent's Catholic Church. In this conflict of loyalties, personal sympathies lie with the Frogtowners, but his/her job tenure depends on getting at least part of what the union officers want.

7. President of Frogtown Residents on Guard, the source of Plan E. This group numbers in its membership about half of the area's residents, and most of the property owners. They strongly desire to remain there and improve it as a family-oriented community. They have held several mass rallies to protest redevelopment plans like Capitol West. Their main theme is that only they have the right to decide what shall be done with their homes and neighborhood. This president is a railroad foreman (or wife of same) who is a lifelong resident of the area, a homeowner at Charles and Farrington. The group might consider Plan C if assurances were given that only the deteriorated houses would be removed. But they see plans A, B, and D as only destroying their neighborhood.

8. Father X of St. Adalberts Catholic Church (or Sister Y, principal of St. Adalberts School). Although the parish is much larger than East Frogtown, the church and school identify closely with their neighborhood and very much want to remain in their present buildings. He/she supports the desires of the local residents, but is also socially conscious enough to want to provide housing opportunities for low-income persons and members of minority groups. The St. Paul Archdiocese has expressed its willingness to finance construction of some housing units for the elderly. The good Father (Sister) wants to negotiate a plan that meets all of these aims as well as possible.

9. The Chairperson of the Planning Council has one, but only one, vote in these deliberations and only as much influence as his/her persuasion powers can gain. He/she is a top assistant to Mayor Latimer and has long experience in Democratic party politics, neighborhood action, and labor-management negotiations. He/she knows that Mayor Latimer privately favors Plan A as offering the most to the city as a whole and to his administration, but hasn't made a public endorsement so as not to bias the work of the Committee. However, this chairperson knows the East Frogtown neighborhood very well from past campaign and organizing experiences. That area split its vote almost evenly in the last mayoral election between Latimer and his more conservative opponent. Being a good politician, this chairperson seeks a solution that alienates as few people as necessary, yet one that will give St. Paul a progressive image and prove to those uppity Minneapolitans that their twin city is living in the 20th century also.

Budget-Making

Russell Brooker
University of Chicago

Overview

This game simulates the role of electoral politics in city budget-making.* It also simulates: (1) the effects of cross-pressures on voters; (2) the detachment of government from the people and the potential for popular alienation from government; and (3) the problems present in a government divided into separate branches with office-holders elected at different times. It has five playing periods and takes from 90 minutes to two hours to play. The necessary materials are: name tags, lists of players and their characteristics, budget-making forms, and a blackboard for keeping score. A computer has been used to simplify score-keeping, but it is not necessary.

The game was designed to be played by undergraduate students but may also be played by graduate students. No special preparation is necessary.

The Players

There are 13 players; each one represents one segment of society. Each player is defined according to his region of town (North, West, or South), his race (white or black), his income (rich, middle, or poor), and his religion (Protestant or Catholic). A player fits into one category of each of four variables. One player may be, for example, a Northern, white, rich Protestant. No two players are exactly alike. The players are named alphabetically for convenience; names begin with letters A through M. See below for the names and characteristics of the players.

There is also a fourteenth player who simulates the press.

Resources

Each player has one vote each playing period. He uses it to elect members of the government. The members of the government draw up the city budget; they have complete control of how the public money is spent.

The Government

There are four members of the government: one Mayor and three Councilmen. All the members of the government are elected by popular vote of

---

*This game was originally played using a computer program written by N. Nuel Wooden of Indiana Central University.

Players' Names and Characteristics

	REGION			RACE		INCOME			RELIGION	
	North	West	South	White	Black	Rich	Middle	Poor	Prot.	Cath.
Adrian	X			X		X			X	
Barney	X			X			X			X
Connie	X			X				X		X
Daphne	X				X	X			X	
Emily	X				X			X		X
Francis		X		X		X				X
Gordon		X			X		X		X	
Hawthorne		X		X			X		X	
Igor		X			X			X	X	
Jay			X	X		X			X	
Kay		X			X	X				X
Lillian		X		X				X	X	
Maxine		X			X			X		X

the 13 players from among the players. The terms of the government members are staggered. The mayor is elected for a two-term period in odd-numbered years; the councilmen are elected for three-period terms. All three Councilmen are elected during the first period but the term of one is for only one period and the term of another is for only two periods. When these shortened terms are over, new elections will be held for full three-period terms.

Making Up the Budget

Each period after elections, the four members of the government move to a separate room and make up the budget. There are two sources of money.

1. Each population-variable is allocated a certain amount of money—usually varying between $50-500. The money is allocated by the director of the game and cannot be spent in other areas. The three councilmen decide by majority vote exactly how the money is spent within the population-variable. For example, if $200 were available to be spent on the basis of income, the Council might decide to spend $100 on rich people and $100 on poor people. The money spent is divided by the number of people in that category; in the example, each rich person would receive $25 ($100/4) and each poor person

would get $20 ($100/5). Players are awarded points rather than dollars; one dollar = one point. (No actual money need be used in this game.) The Council repeats this process for all four population-variables. The Council may not spend more money than it has or save money from period to period.

2. The other source of money is that which the Mayor has at his disposal. He is given approximately $100 each period. He may spend the money any way he pleases. He may spent it all on rich people or divide it equally among all ten population-categories. He may or may not coordinate his spending with the Council's—as he pleases. Scoring of his expenditures is done exactly the same as the Council's.

Scoring

Before voting for the government is conducted, all the players are informed of approximately how much money will be available to the government. For example, the available money might be:

Council:	Region	$300	Mayor: $100
	Race	$200	
	Income	$250	
	Religion	$100	

After the Council and the Mayor allocate the money (a time limit of about 10 minutes should be used), each population-category's score is figured by the game director. The totals might be:

North	85
West	70
South	60
.	
.	
.	
Catholic	50

These are the only numbers the other nine players are given. The nongovernmental players are never given any other information about how the government is working; they must rely on the stories of the government members and the press.

After receiving the scores of each population category, each player figures his score by adding the scores of his four categories. For example, a northern black, poor Protestant would add the four scores for: North + Black + Poor + Protestant.

Course of the Game

At the beginning of each period elections are held. (All four government members are elected during the first period—after that one Councilman and, in odd-numbered periods, a Mayor are elected.)

After the election, the four government members move to another room. They are accompanied by the player representing the press.

The government then spends the money it has available. (Play money may be used, but it would be easier to use accounting forms, such as the one below.)

Budget-Making Form

	Council	Mayor		Category Scores	
Region					
North	_____ +	_____ =	_____ ÷	= _____	North
West	_____ +	_____ =	_____ ÷	= _____	West
South	_____ +	_____ =	_____ ÷	= _____	South
Race					
White	_____ +	_____ =	_____ ÷	= _____	White
Black	_____ +	_____ =	_____ ÷	= _____	Black
Income					
Rich	_____ +	_____ =	_____ ÷	= _____	Rich
Middle class	_____ +	_____ =	_____ ÷	= _____	Middle
Poor	_____ +	_____ =	_____ ÷	= _____	Poor
Religion					
Protestant	_____ +	_____ =	_____ ÷	= _____	Protestant
Catholic	_____ +	_____ =	_____ ÷	= _____	Catholic

↑
The nongovernmental people see only these numbers.

The other players are then informed of the scores of each population-category. The government and the press return to the same room as the other players. If the non-government players want to learn what happened in the other room, they must ask the press or the government members. The press is required to basically tell the truth; the government members are under no restrictions whatever concerning honesty.

Scores for each player are determined and new elections are held. This process goes on five periods. The player with the highest score at the end of the game is the winner. (In order to avoid end-of-game problems, the players could be told the game will last six periods.)

Changes in the Rules

Several modifications or changes could be made in these rules:

(1) The money allocated to the population-variables may change greatly. For example, the money allocated to Income could increase drastically as the game

progresses. If this happened, the players would divide more and more on the basis of income—simulating an increase in class consciousness. A sample of how the money allocations might change is:

Dollars Allocated

Period	Variable				
	Region	Race	Income	Religion	Mayor
1	$400	$350	$ 50	$370	$100
2	390	330	100	350	90
3	320	330	200	320	110
4	290	280	400	200	90
5	140	100	800	130	100

(2) Provision can be made for corruption. The government players can be given play money to spend and be allowed to give money to individuals including themselves. Each dollar would then equal one point. Any money spent in this way would have to be made public so that the nongovernmental players could see it. But if a government player surreptitiously kept money for himself, it would be added to his score. If he were caught by another government player or by the press player, his dishonesty could be exposed to the other players.

Provisions for a "recall rule" should be included if this rule is used; for example, nine of the 13 votes could be enough to remove a corrupt office-holder from his position of trust.

(3) Councilmen could be elected by region rather than at large. Regional elections would open the possibility for gerrymandering. Players could be changed from one region to another during the game. (With only 13 players election-at-large is probably the better way to play, but with 17 or more, regional elections would be better.)

Comments

Post-game discussions should include questions about the realism of the game. How are budget-making processes in the real world different? Does this game really simulate actual budget-making processes, or is it more of an analogy for all authoritative allocation processes which include, but are not limited to, budget-making?

The game could be used to study the problems or responsibility and accountability in government. Did the members of the government feel they should be accountable to the people who elected them, to all the people, or did they only want to pad their own scores? Did office-holders suddenly become much more responsible just before they came up for re-election? How did the players handle the problems of cross-pressures? For example, if a Council member were elected by a coalition of poor and middle-income people, how did he vote in budgeting money on the basis of religion or race? How did the players deal with the lack of reliable information? Did they become cynical or behave irrationally? Were conscientious office-holders defeated for re-election because the voters had no way to tell who to hold accountable? If so, how did the defeated office-holders react? Did players work together by forming lasting coalitions or political parties? On the whole, what effect did a distant and divided government have on the accountability of the office-holders in the game? What effect does it have in the real world?

A fifteenth player, who would act as a political scientist, could be added. He would observe and analyze play in the game. Two political scientists could be used; one would stay with the non-governmental players, and the other would observe all the government sessions. After the game, they would write separate analytical "articles" to be read by all the game's participants. Criticisms of these "articles" would be discussed along with the problems of political scientists and the dangers of specialization in academic fields.

Slate-Making

Russell Brooker
University of Chicago

Overview

This game simulates the process of making electoral slates by political parties in a large ethnically diverse city. It has three playing periods and takes approximately 90 minutes to play overall. The only materials needed are: name tags, play money, index cards to serve as vote tokens, ballot boxes, slate-making forms, and a blackboard for keeping score.

The game was designed for undergraduate students but may also be played by graduate students. No special preparation is needed, but a knowledge of urban politics would help make the game more interesting.

The Players

There are eight ethnic groups, each represented by one player. They are:

1. Black
2. WASP
3. Italian
4. Irish
5. Polish
6. Latino
7. Croatian
8. Jewish

More players could be added (e.g., Slovenian, Lithuanian), some could be deleted, or teams of players could represent each ethnic group.

There are also two political parties, each represented by one player or one team of players. They are:

1. The Socially Oriented Activist Party (SOAP)
2. The American Party of Excellence (APE)

Two games go on simultaneously, with two winners. All the ethnic groups compete against each other, and each political party competes against the other. One ethnic group wins, and one party wins. The ethnic groups are indifferent to the successes or failures of the parties, and the parties are indifferent to the fates of the ethnic groups.

The Slate

Each party completes a slate of 16 offices to be chosen in an election. The offices are listed on the Slate-Making Form. Each party must slate an ethnic group representative for each office. There are no restrictions on which ethnic groups can be slated or how many offices an ethnic group may be slated for. For example, SOAP could legally slate Jews for every office, or an Italian could be slated for Mayor by both parties.

Four offices are filled by election each playing period. They are:

1. Mayor
2. Assessor
3. Clerk
4. Prosecutor

The other 12 offices are filled by appointment. These offices, however, must be slated before the election each period. When one official is elected, all the subordinate candidates running on his party slate are also chosen. For example: if the APE Mayor were elected, the APE candidates for Park Commissioner, Police Chief, and Fire Chief would automatically be chosen.

Object of the Game

All ten players want to win patronage jobs. Each office carries with it some jobs. The Mayor, for example, has 300 jobs at his disposal, while the Criminal Attorney has only 80. Each job can be considered a "point." Each ethnic group wins the patronage jobs for each office he is selected to fill, whether he is chosen by election or by appointment. Each party wins the patronage jobs that its candidates have won. For example, if the APE candidate for Mayor and his appointive offices were:

		Jobs
Mayor	Black	300
Park Commissioner	WASP	200
Police Chief	WASP	150
Fire Chief	Italian	100

and the APE candidate won the Mayor's office, the black player gets 300 jobs, the WASP player 350 jobs, and the Italian player 100 jobs. The APE player would win 750 jobs (300 + 200 + 150 + 100).

The game lasts three playing periods; each player's scores for all three periods are added at the end of the game. One ethnic group and one party will win with more jobs won than their competitors.

Resources

Each ethnic group has two resources—votes and money. Each vote is marked for the office it is good for—i.e., Mayor, Assessor, Clerk, or Prosecutor. Each vote is good only for the office which is marked. Votes are also marked for each playing period; and are good only for one period; they may not be saved. Money may be spent on any office and may be saved, although any money still held by players at the end of the game will have no value. Resources are not distributed equally. Some ethnic groups have more votes and money. The approximate resources of each player are listed on the Slate-Making Form. The actual number of resources held by each ethnic group should be changed each period.

Elections are conducted at the end of each period. There are four separate

Slate-Making Form

Party_____

Period_____

OFFICES		PATRONAGE Jobs	SLATE
Elected	Appointed		
Mayor		300	_____
	Park Commissioner	200	_____
	Police Chief	150	_____
	Fire Chief	100	_____
City Assessor		200	_____
	City Inspector	150	_____
	City Auditor	100	_____
	City Accountant	50	_____
City Clerk		200	_____
	Patronage Director	180	_____
	Election Director	70	_____
City Prosecutor		200	_____
	Criminal Attorney	80	_____
	Civil Attorney	60	_____
	Bright Young Lawyer No. 1	30	_____
	Bright Young Lawyer No. 2	30	_____

Approximate Number of Votes and Money:

	Votes	Money		Votes	Money
Black	4	10	Irish	3	45
WASP	1	60	Latino	2	10
Polish	3	40	Croatian	1	20
Italian	2	30	Jewish	1	30

elections. The ethnic groups give their votes and money to the candidates they wish to vote for. Elections are conducted in this way: Each candidate's votes and money are multiplied and the product is compared to his opponent's; the candidate with the larger product wins the election. For example:

	Votes	x	Money	=	Election Score
APE Mayor Candidate (WASP)	20		$35		700
SOAP Mayor Candidate (Polish)	15		$40		600

In this election, the APE candidate (WASP) would become Mayor and the APE candidates for Park Commissioner, Police Chief, and Fire Chief would also be chosen. The WASP player would then win 300 jobs, the three subordinate candidates would win their patronage jobs, and the APE party player would win the jobs for all four offices.

Four elections are conducted each period—for Mayor, Assessor, Clerk, and Prosecutor. Each election is conducted the same way. It is at the ethnic groups' discretion how they wish to allocate their votes and money.

The political parties have no resources other than their power to slate ethnic groups for office.

Third Parties

Any disaffected ethnic group or groups can form a third party and run its own candidates for office. To provide for this eventuality, a Democratic American Party badge—DAP—may be included in the game. The third party, or any other party, need not slate nominations for all offices; it could, for example, slate only the Prosecutor's office. If there are three or more candidates running for the same office, the highest election score wins the election, whether or not it is a majority of the scores. Fourth or fifth parties may, of course, be formed the same way.

Party Resources

If desired, party players may be given their own resources. Doing this would give the party players some autonomy and could result in the development of an invulnerable machine, on the model of the Democratic machine in Chicago. An easy way to give the parties resources would be to give each party $50 each period.

A better, but more complicated way, would be to give the parties resources contingent on their winning offices. That is, with each office, the victorious party would receive votes and money as well as patronage jobs. An example of how this could be done is:

	Jobs	Votes	Money
Mayor	300	4	$100
Assessor	200	4	75
Clerk	200	4	50
Prosecutor	200	4	25

Further Comments

In playing the game, the Game Director should be sure to change the resources of each ethnic group each period; doing this will keep the party players alert, trying to determine who has the most power at any particular time. There could be a pattern to the changes; for example, the Croatians could get stronger each period while the WASPs grow weaker.

After each game, several questions about the players' rationality and styles of play could be discussed. For example: Did the parties slate the most powerful ethnic groups for the best offices? Did they construct well-balanced slates? Did they notice when one ethnic group's resources rose or fell suddenly and take advantage of changes? Did the parties organize the coalitions, or did the ethnic groups organize themselves? Did some ethnic groups side with one party, or did everybody play as a free agent?

Questions about the realism of the game should also be discussed. Do real politicians go through similar processes in balancing tickets? Are the votes and money in the game similar to the resources in the real world? Is ethnic balancing the same process as geographical or ideological balancing? Do groups in the real world get rewarded entirely on the basis of what they contribute to electoral victories, or are there other criteria?

The main processes simulated in the game are slate-making by party chieftains and coalition formation by ethnic groups, but it could also be used to simulate party-formation by dispensing with the separate party players. The ethnic groups would then be forced to put together their own slates. Play would probably be more unstable and third party threats more common as coalitions argued over distribution of offices. The two versions could be played by the same players and then compared to each other and to the real world.

An additional player, who would simulate a political scientist, could be added to the game. His job would be to observe and then analyze the game to the participants. They, in turn, would make comments on his accuracy and insight. Problems of political scientists could then be discussed.

Precinct Caucus Simulation

Ann Wynia
North Hennepin Community College

Anne Walcott
Gustavus Adolphus College

Subject Matter: Political participation.

Appropriate Course and Level: American Government, State and Local Government, Urban Government.

Description of Context: Although the context is the precinct caucus, a lower level form of party organization, this simulation could apply to any situation which would involve a somewhat formal meeting and decision-making. This simulation then involves two levels of learning: (1) knowledge and understanding of the precinct caucus and various other levels of party organization in Minnesota; and (2) an introduction to the uses of parliamentary procedure and the technical aspects of conducting formal meetings. Since political parties generally have meetings at least to decide who shall run the party and to create a platform, this simulation could be adapted to any state's party organization.

The problems to be solved by the members of the precinct caucus include: the election of a permanent chairperson, the election of a precinct chairperson who will run the party at the precinct level for the next year, the election of two election judges who will count votes, the election of delegates and alternates who will subsequently attend the next party level convention (which in the case of Minnesota has the power to endorse candidates for political office at appropriate levels), the debate of issues and their approval by members of the caucus by majority vote. These issues then go to the next party convention for inclusion in a platform.

Number of Players: There should be probably at least ten players.

Number of Roles and Brief Description:

1. Convenor of the meeting. This is a temporary role until the permanent Chair is elected. This player calls the meeting to order and calls for the election of a permanent chair by majority vote.
2. Permanent Chair. This is a demanding role since the student should have some knowledge of parliamentary procedure. If there is no one in the class that has this experience, the instructor should fill this role.
3. Parliamentarian. Again, ideally, a student should have experience in this field. However, this role can be combined with the chair and played by the instructor, or someone outside of the class who has the requisite qualifications.
4. Election judges. The only qualification here is an ability to count!

Length of Time Required: The minimum time required would be one 50-minute class period. This simulation can run indefinitely depending on the number of issues discussed and the number of alternates and delegates that need to be elected. Alternates and delegates need not be included in the simulation, particularly if they are not an important element in the party organization.

How Many Distinct Periods, and How Long They Last: There are really no distinct periods unless one considers the problems to be solved as periods. Except for election of delegates and alternates and the debate of issues, the other problems should not take more than five minutes. The debate of issues usually takes a long time and is best not controlled by the instructor. The frustration felt by simulation participants when there is no time left and they have not accomplished as much as they would like is fairly realistic. Here it is good to point out that although the use of parliamentary procedure can facilitate the running of meetings it can also because of its democratic nature frustrate those who feel efficiency is a priority goal.

Physical and/or Computational Facilities Required: It is best for this simulation to have a large room with movable chairs and tables. A blackboard is also helpful to record candidates and to list issues if they have not been duplicated for each participant. The size of the room and the need for flexible arrangements depends on how large the class is. If you have 10-30 members you may not need movable tables and chairs. If, on the other hand, you have a class of 80 or more you may wish to divide them into two or more groups.

How Much and How Long Must Participants Prepare: This is very flexible. You can conduct this game with no prior preparation—just start the meeting! Obviously, the instructor must be knowledgeable on the subject of procedure and to some extent his/her own party organization. If it is desired, the participants can be required to read a special handout on parliamentary procedure (Appendix A) and handouts discussing various election procedures used by the local parties (Appendices B and C). The instructor can also assign various books and articles on parliamentary procedure and the conduct of meetings. The students may also be required to develop issues beforehand that they will present for debate. Substantive material may be required reading as background to these issues.

Specific students may be asked to prepare to be the chairperson and parliamentarian.

If you do require preparation, it might be advisable to conduct a short quiz.

Evaluation: We do not advise evaluation on the quality of participation. However, there should be "points" (which may translate into grades) given for attendance and the presentation of an issue. If prior preparation is required, points can be also given for a short quiz.

APPENDIX A
Parliamentary Procedures at a Glance

To Do This:[1]	You Say This:	May You Interrupt Speaker?	Must You Be Seconded?	Is the Motion Debatable?	Is the Motion Amendable?	What Vote Is Required?
Adjourn the meeting	"I move that we adjourn."	No	Yes	No	No	Majority vote required
Recess the meeting	"I move that we recess until. . ."	No	Yes	No	Yes	Majority required
Complain about noise, room temperature, etc.	"Point of privilege."	Yes	No	No[2]	No	No vote required[3]
Suspend further consideration of something	"I move we table it."	No	Yes	No	No	Majority required
End debate	"I move the previous question."	No	Yes	No	No	Two-thirds vote required
Postpone consideration of something	"I move we postpone this matter until. . ."	No	Yes	Yes	Yes	Majority required
Have something studied further	"I move we refer this matter to a committee."	No	Yes	Yes	Yes	Majority required
Amend a motion	"I move that this motion be amended by. . ."	No	Yes	Yes	Yes	Majority required
Introduce business (a primary motion)	"I move that. . ."	No	Yes	Yes	Yes	Majority required

[1]The motions or points above are listed in established order of precedence. When any one of them is pending you may not introduce another that is listed below it, but you may introduce another that is listed above it.

[2]In this case, any resulting motion is debatable.

[3]Chair decides.

APPENDIX A. Parliamentary Procedures at a Glance (continued)

To Do This:[1]	You Say This:	May You Interrupt Speaker?	Must You Be Seconded?	Is the Motion Debatable?	Is the Motion Amendable?	What Vote Is Required?
Object to procedure or to a personal affront.	"Point of order."	Yes	No	No	No	No vote required: Chair decides
Request information	"Point of information."	Yes, if urgent	No	No	No	No vote required
Ask for a vote by actual count to verify a voice vote	"I call for a division of the house."	No[2]	No	No	No	No vote required unless someone objects[3]
Object to considering some undiplomatic or improper matter	"I object to consideration of this question."	Yes	No	No	No	Two-thirds vote required
Take up a matter previously tabled	"I move we take from the table. . ."	No	Yes	No	No	Majority required
Reconsider something already disposed of	"I move we now (or later) reconsider our action relative to. . ."	Yes	Yes	Yes[4]	No	Majority required
Consider something out of its scheduled order	"I move we suspend the rules and consider. . ."	No	Yes	No	No	Two-thirds vote required
Vote on a ruling by the chair	"I appeal the chair's decision."	Yes	Yes	Yes	No	Majority required

[1]The actions, points, and proposals listed above have no established order of precedence. Any of them may be induced at any time—except when the meeting is considering one of the top three matters listed on page 1 (motion to adjourn, motion to recess, point of privilege).
[2]But divisions must be called for before another motion is started.
[3]Then majority vote is required.
[4]If original motion is debatable.

APPENDIX B
The Hare System

Explanation and Sample Ballot
Questions and Answers

Instructions: Rank as many candidates as you like. Indicate your first choice by the number (1), and so on.

Question 1: Is a number 1 vote weakened by the addition of the numbers?
Answer: No.

Question 2: Just how does the Hare system work?
Answer:

(1) The *first* step in counting ballots is to assign *all* ballots to the candidates according to the number 1 preference indicated, and to count the ballots for each candidate.

(2) In terms of the total number of valid ballots cast and the number of positions to be filled, the mininum number of votes necessary to insure election is computed. This number is called a *quota.*

(3) Any candidate with at least as many ballots as the quota is declared elected. A set of his ballots equal in number to the quota and selected at random are set aside (and never used again), and any excess ballots are "distributed" according to the number 2 votes.

(4) When at any stage no remaining candidate has enough votes to satisfy the quota, the one with the smallest number is declared eliminated, and his ballots are distributed among the other remaining candidates.

(5) This process is repeated until the requisite number of candidates is elected.

Question 3: How far should one go in writing numbers 1, 2, etc.?

Answer: The farther the better, since it is possible that even numbers beyond the number of positions to be filled will enter into the outcome. There are two limiting considerations; the extent of the voter's acqaintance with the qualifications of the candidates, and the fact that the only way to make sure that a ballot cannot be counted for a candidate the voter opposes is not to assign that candidate any preference-number.

Question 4: Does the Hare system have any outstanding advantages?

Answer: The principal objective is contained in the words *proportional representation.* A minority group, for example, having at least as many votes as the quota can guarantee election of its representatives.

Sample Ballot (16 to be elected)

(18) Bach	(4) Sophocles	(23) Marx
(11) Beethoven	(27) Voltaire	(8) Plato
(22) Goethe	(13) Archimedes	(17) Livy
(10) Homer	(7) Buffon	(1) Jefferson
(3) Michelangelo	(28) Darwin	(9) Boas
(29) Rodin	(20) Galileo	(6) Confucius
(12) Schopenhauer	(24) Lucretius	(14) Freud
(5) Praxiteles	(15) Mendel	(21) Greeley
(19) Shakespeare	(2) Pasteur	(25) Herodotus
(16) Socrates	(26) Malthus	

APPENDIX C
The Iowa Sub-Caucus System of Proportional Voting for the Selection of Delegates

The Iowa sub-caucus system essentially enables voters to group (caucus) according to either candidate preference, issue position, or any other identifying characteristic for the purpose of allocating delegates to be selected by each individual caucus. The number of delegates allocated to each caucus is calculated by determining the proportion of voters in the caucus to the total number of voters present and voting. This proportion or percentage is then multiplied by the total number of delegates to receive the number of delegates to be allocated to each caucus.

Example: Given—100 voters   10 possible delegates

> 10 = number of voters in Caucus A
> 30 = number of voters in Caucus B
> 60 = number of voters in Caucus C
> ___
> 100 = total voters

Step 1: Caucus A = 10/100 or 1/10
Caucus B = 30/100 or 3/10
Caucus C = 60/100 or 3/5

Step 2: Caucus A = 1/10 x 10 = 1 delegate
Caucus B = 3/10 x 10 = 3 delegates
Caucus C = 3/5 x 10 = 6 delegates
___
10 delegates (total)

The method of electing delegates within the caucus is generally left up to each caucus to decide for itself.

APPENDIX D
Limited Voting

Under limited voting, each person voting may cast one vote for every two delegate positions to be filled. When the number is not evenly divisible by two, each voter shall be entitled to one additional vote. A plurality shall be sufficient to elect.

The Aristotle Game*

Roberta Ann Johnson
University of California, Santa Cruz (visiting)

Use in conjunction with Aristotle's *The Politics,* Books III and IV. Designed for an introduction to political science course. Requires a regular classroom with movable chairs and enough room between groups that they don't interfere with each other.

Goals: Behavioral

1. To create a more relaxed classroom atmosphere
2. To create a situation where students teach each other
3. To get students personally involved in politicking

Cognitive

1. To get students to read *The Politics,* Books III and IV
2. To get students to think about and remember some of the strengths and weaknesses of the different forms of government

Recommended Roles:

> 3 former slaves
> 6 laborers and artisans (middle class)
> 5 farmers (middle class)
> 4 "of good birth" aristocracy
> 5 very wealthy
> 1 the richest
> 1 the most "virtuous," best educated, most "noble"

(The numbers for each category can be adjusted depending on class size, but general proportions must be respected so that those arguing for democracy, usually the middle class and former slaves, must outnumber the others.)

---

*A special thanks to the following San Francisco State University students for their help in improving this simple simulation: Doris Godinez-Taylor, Ben A. Van Horn, Loretta MacDonald, Marcia Beck, David Sanford, Mary Rassette.

Recommended Class Size: 25-40 students.

Reading Assignment: Assign the Aristotle reading a week before describing and assigning roles for the game.

Role Requirements: The task assigned is to prepare statements in defense of a particular system of government. The simulated role they play also includes the ability to influence others with resources. The instructor should not have to make this second aspect of their role explicit.

Role Assignments: A combination of self-selecting and assigning. Third World students, for example, usually want to play former slaves. I recommend that you assign the role of at least some "aristocrats" to class-talkers who are usually very well prepared for class. The impact of the educated aristocrats argument will be best felt if it comes from the most articulate and prepared students. If possible, the "richest" person should be played by an aggressive wheeler-dealer type student. I chose to play the role of the most noble. There is an enormous responsibility attached to that choice. In my opinion, teacher-participation will only work if teacher-student formal barriers have been broken down already so that student and teacher will feel comfortable arguing against each other energetically and unself-consciously. If the teacher participates, then there needs to be another way of timing presentations besides teacher responsibility. I recommend a kitchen timer. It must be noted that many students prefer the instructor to participate as a referee, not a player.

Incentives to Prepare and Play Well: Teacher evaluation, peer group pressure, commitment to the game.

Recommended Time:

Two hours	
10 minutes	10-minute preparation
30 minutes	5-minute presentations from each group
10 minutes	10-minute break
30 minutes	5-minute rebuttals from each group
5 minutes	5-minute break
	Vote
	De-briefing

Seating: The class is seated in two ways:

1. They sit in groups for preparation. This emphasizes group solidarity and membership.

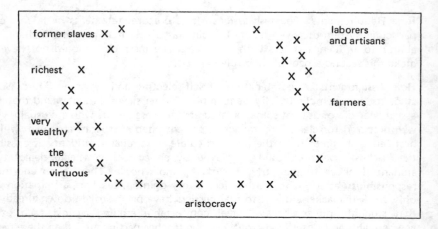

2. They sit in a circle simulating a polis for presentation.

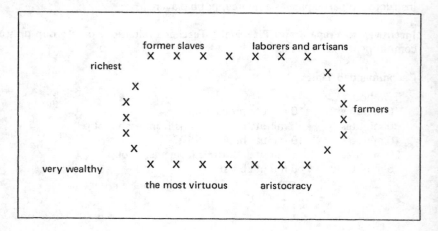

The Game: Each having prepared at home, the class has 10 minutes class time to finalize their presentation (decide who speaks first, etc.). Then each group presents arguments for five minutes. The former slaves usually decide to argue for democracy and that gives the pro-democracy group 10 minutes for their presentation.

There is a 10-minute break during which time some people prepare rebuttals, some go out into the hall and there is lots of talking within and between groups. This is an essential feature of the game.

When the polis reconvenes, each group rebuts the specific arguments of the others. It is their last chance to make their form of government look like the best form.

At the end of the arguments there is a five-minute break (more talking and moving around) and then a vote is called.

Goals Achieved and Unforeseen Benefits: The Aristotle Game is a lively, exciting event for student and teacher. The interaction is formal argument and informal talking, organizing and politicking. The students are responding to each other and trying to persuade each other. In their formal presentations they are getting eye contact with each other, not just with me, and the goal of students teaching each other is achieved.

I am continually amazed at how well the students prepare and how well they play the game. Even those who have been quiet all semester say something because of the more open atmosphere of the class, because I am there evaluating their performance and because of peer evaluation. How well their presentations go seems to be separate from the issue of whether they get the votes in the end. The goal, for most of the game is to do justice to the form of government they are defending. They take their responsibilities very seriously.

The game, according to the students themselves, made the reading more valuable, memorable, and less "tedious."

Students read the assignment carefully, not only for their own arguments but also to be able to answer the other groups. They have an incentive to read the entire assignment carefully and thoughtfully. An unforeseen benefit was that they learned to appreciate metaphors, Aristotle's images (Antisthenes fable, flute-playing, mixing coarse food with refined food, etc.) because they not only had to use them, but they had to be able to turn them around against other users. They did so with a great deal of zeal and imagination. This aspect of their presentations provides humor and fun. Not only are students prepared but they learn about the poetry of political science, the joy of a metaphor. Students talked to and mingled with other students they hadn't talked to before. This they all say is a great advantage to playing the game.

But the game does more than just achieve the behavioral and cognitive goals outlined in the beginning.

1. Students learn about the importance of the public display in the polis. It made them feel pressured and less inclined they said to break with their group and vote for another.

2. Students learn that politicking is more important than arguments. The outcome of the vote is usually the result of what happens during the breaks *not* how good their arguments were. The important lesson of politics which they will never forget because of this experience was that it was bargaining and personalities which determined the final vote not commitment to principle.

3. Students learn that mere numbers aren't all that matters. In the beginning of the game it looked like there would be a democracy and no one would believe me if I claimed that people would vote to disenfranchise themselves—to decide not to have influence in government—but that is, in fact, what has happened.

Thus, an unforeseen benefit is that the Aristotle Game teaches a modern lesson of politics—people are more moved by bargains struck than principles believed and one-person-one-vote is less important than the resources we have to bargain with.

Zorax

James A. Blessing
Susquehanna University

Subject Matter: Classical Political Philosophy—version A stresses historical political philosophy; version B stresses normative political philosophy based on historical study.

Course Level: Upper level.

Context: Conference or convention to develop a constitutional basis for a political system; i.e., to form a social contract.

Number of Players: Minimum—4-5; Maximum—12-14, though it could be larger.

Number of Roles: Minimum—4-5; Maximum—6-7, though it could be larger. (With larger number of roles, best to have two or more people jointly play one role as delegates of that philosophic position.)

Nature of Roles: Version A—Plato, Aristotle, Machiavelli, Locke and Hobbes; others can be added (Historical). Version B—Individuals play themselves; their own positions (Normative). In both versions they are trustees rather than delegates of a position.

Optional Roles: Chairperson can be one of participants or instructor. Any of the roles can be deleted; more roles (philosophers) can be added.

Length of Time: Minimum—two hours; Maximum—open ended. Recommended time—four hours in two two-hour blocks.

Periods: Two hours: (1) Orientation and selection of chairperson; (2) Presentation of basic positions and proposals; (3) clarification of areas of agreement and disagreement. Two hours: (4) Negotiations within group and sub-groups re areas of disagreement to reach optimally unanimous consent to a social contract or 2/3-3/4 agreement as to nature of system to be established.

Facilities: Seminar room or regular classroom is sufficient.

Preparation by Participants: Each participant (or pairs or trios if more than one representing a particular position) must prepare a *position paper* stating views and supporting arguments re: (1) Meta physics or view of reality; (2) Epistemology or theory of knowledge about reality; (3) View of human nature; (4) Statement of goals based on first three points; and (5) Statement of means based on first four points.

In version A, the position papers would reflect view of a particular political philosopher, such as Plato or Locke. In version B, the position paper would reflect the normative view of the participant.

Special Materials: None except name tags if a large number of students.

Special Features: Number of roles and players is flexible. Small number of roles-players provide conference simulation; large number provides convention simulation.

Can be used to teach-review either historical political philosophy (version A) or normative political philosophy (version B).

Depth of subject matter is also variable.

Special Note: This simulation works best at the end of a course in political philosophy.

Comments: This simulation has two versions. Version A is in the context of historical political philosophy and version B is in the context of normative political philosophy. The substantive objective of version A is to provide students with a means and purpose for learning in detail the arguments of a particular political philosopher. The substantive objective of version B is to encourage students, based on study in the course, to develop their own philosophic position about the nature of and reasons for a desired political (socioeconomic) system.

In both versions the students not only must learn or develop a philosophic position but they also must argue or debate other positions during which they experience the negotiating process and gain a greater appreciation of the complexity of developing a consensus out of different views or interests.

The major advantages of this simulation at the end of the course are that it adds a "purpose" to studying the material and provides a little excitement—something not always present in the study of classical political philosophy. The students appear to "get into it" and they have stated that they enjoy it and that it serves as an incentive to learn the material since they will be "on display." Finally, it does serve as a good summary-review or conclusion to the course—and it is best used at the end of the course.

The rules have purposely been kept simple and to a minimum—they are to accomplish the points stipulated in the outline of periods (see above) and they are to function as "trustees" of their position (not delegates). This is necessary so they have flexibility to negotiate. These rules, however, could easily be made more explicit to suit the instructor's own purpose or time constraints.

In a small class I allow the participants to select their own roles (in version A—it is not relevant in version B), though this itself often involves some negotiation. I have also found it best if the instructor function as chairperson (a little more order and efficiency can be maintained).

The information presented above under periods of activity and preparation outline what is to be done. In period two each role presents an oral synopsis of its proposal and in period three the group identifies the areas of agreement and disagreement. In period four the areas of disagreement and the reasons for such are discussed (or debated) and then negotiated by the group and/or subgroups until a unanimous consensus is reached, a 2/3 or 3/4 agreement is reached, or an impasse becomes evident. At this point the group must draw up an outline of this agreed upon social contract (or contracts if an impasse between subgroups was reached). After this there is a combined review-debriefing session focusing on why they did or did not reach a consensus, making reference to substantive argument and problem encountered as well as procedural-negotiating problems. Finally the debriefing concludes with a discussion of whether or not the simulation was of any benefit in increasing their understanding of the substantive data and the problems associated with trying to develop a consensus or compromise out of differing positions or interests.

Latin American Nation-State Simulation

Gary W. Wynia
University of Minnesota

Rules and Instructions

This game seeks to simulate the issue area conflict and bargaining processes of Latin American political systems. Individuals representing different interests and groups will contest for the control of government and the promulgation of public policies. The goal of each player is the satisfaction of his/her own and his/her constituents' interests.

I. Basic Concepts

A. *Power Points.* Each player is assigned a number of points to represent power resources. These power points are the currency used to compute victory and defeat on particular issue conflicts, and are exchanged as a result of policy decisions.

B. *Government.* The government is controlled by the individual or coalition of players that secures a plurality of power points in any contest for control of government. Control over the government gains the right to propose *three consecutive issues* for consideration.

C. *Coalition.* Any player may form a coalition with others in order to contest any issue as long as its membership in the coalition does not violate its role definition. Coalitions are formed to contest control of government and to contest issues.

II. Basic Activities

The game consists of competition among players over the control of government and over the passage and implementation of policies. The basic steps in the game consist of: (1) election of a government, (2) voting on issues, (3) implementing policy by avoiding policy blockage, coups, or revolts.

III. General Format

A government will be elected and given the opportunity to propose *three* (3) issues in succession before a new election must be called. Each issue will be debated and voted on after which opponents can try to block the policy. If the opponents succeed, the government must reconsider it or move to another issue; if they fail to block, the policy will be considered implemented and the appropriate points will be redistributed among other players.

IV. Electing a Government

A. Any individual or coalition of *domestic* players may be a candidate. Their announcement must be accompanied by an oral statement of their positions on any three issues of their choice.

B. A ten minute "campaign" will be conducted in which all players will be free to consult with each other; at any time before the election any player may announce that he has decided to join one of the competing slates if invited by that slate to do so.

C. *Voter eligibility:* All players except the foreign industrialist, Russian ambassador, American ambassador, and military may cast all of their power points in an election. The foreign industrialist may cast only ¼ of his points, the American ambassador may cast only ¼ of his points, and all branches of the military may cast ¼ of their points.

D. The slate that receives the greatest *plurality* of power points will be declared the new government. Upon taking office it will acquire a bonus of five government points that it may use on issue voting only. They are left in the government and are not taken by a departing coalition if it is replaced by another.

E. Once elected, a coalition will offer three issues, one-by-one, for consideration before having to face a new election. The only exception is the overthrow of the government by a military coup which leads to either a military government or a new election.

V. Voting on Issues

A. Before each announcement of an issue the government will have five minutes to design its issue. If it fails to submit an issue on time, each member of the coalition must give up one point. This will be repeated for every additional five-minute delay.

B. The government will announce the issue and its power point redistribution after which there will be five minutes of negotiations.

C. After negotiations a vote will be taken with all players except foreigners and the military eligible to cast all of their points. *Foreign players* and all branches of the *military* may cast only half of their points when voting on issues. An issue requires a plurality to pass.

VI. Popular Initiative Through Public Protests

A. A government may be forced to take up an issue if its opponents can gain 1/3 or 33 of the total game power points to support an initiative. If this occurs, the government must propose the issue for consideration within five minutes; the government will define the issue and select the power point distribution included in it. This will count as one of the three issues permitted a government between elections.

VII. Blocking

A. After an issue has passed, any player may seek to block its implementation. After a block is called for, there will be five minutes of negotiations after which the proponent of the block may or may not call for a vote. If a vote is called, the blocking section must receive 40 power points in order to succeed. If it fails, the leader of the block will forfeit one point to the government which must allocate it to one of the coalition members.

B. If the block succeeds, the government must consider the issue again (it is free to change its original point redistribution) or move to another issue.

VIII. Coups

A. The military may carry out a coup at any time. When any branch announces an intention to coup, all other activities will stop and there will be five minutes of negotiations. If the military calls for a vote, it will then be taken to determine the success of the coup. If it does not call for a vote, the game will be resumed where it was interrupted.

B. To succeed, the coup must receive 33 power points, or a total equal to one-third of the game's total points.

C. If the coup succeeds, the military may implement one policy, redistributing up to ten points among players. It may take up two additional issues, but must submit each to a vote following regular procedures. Then, like all governments, it must call an election.

D. If the coup fails, those branches of the military leading it will sacrifice one point each to the government.

IX. Revolts

A. Either the *peasants* or the *labor movement* can lead a revolt against the government. To succeed they must receive 40 power points.

B. If the revolt succeeds, either the peasant leader or the labor leader may form a new government and consider three issues. Or, if they wish, they may call for new elections.

C. If the revolt fails, the peasant and/or labor leaders must give up a point to the government.

X. Bonus or Success Points

A. Whenever a government secures the passage *and* the implementation of an issue, it will receive one extra point that it may use *only* on issue voting.

B. Bonus points are good only while the coalition that won them is in office; they disappear at the end of a government's three issue tenure. That is, after each election the government starts with zero success points.

XI. Crises

A. Immediately before the government announces an issue, it must pick a card from the "crisis deck." Half of the cards in the deck will be blank; the other half will contain crisis issues to which the government must respond before taking up its next issue. The crisis issue is not included within the total of three issues permitted a government between elections.

XII. Special Considerations

A. The American Ambassador and Russian Ambassador have five extra "aid points" which they may give to a government or take away after they are given. The points, however, are used only by the government and cannot be kept by individual players.

B. The foreign investor has three extra "bribe" points that he may give to any contender in the government. The points will be kept by the player when he leaves the government.

Power Contenders

Power Points	Contender
5	Hacendado Farmer
7	Urban Middle Sectors
9	Urban Labor
9	Peasants
5	Domestic Industrialist
4	Archbishop
4	Student Leader
4	Conservative Party
7	Christian Democratic Party
5	Socialist Party
4	Communist Party
10	Army
6	Navy
6	Air Force
6	U.S. Ambassador
4	Soviet Ambassador
5	Foreign Investor

Country Profile

Population: 24 million

Class Structure:

Rural Upper	2%
Urban Upper	8%
Rural Middle	10%
Urban Middle	15%
Rural Lower	40%
Urban Lower	25%

Land Distribution:
Upper 2% own 60% of land
Middle 10% own 30% of land
Lower 50% own 10% of land

Gross National Product Distribution:

Agriculture	40%
Mining	20%
Industry	15%
Services	25%

Exports to:

United States	40%
West Germany	20%
Japan	10%
Great Britain	10%
Latin America	8%
Others	12%

Size: 500,000 square miles

Literacy: 60%

Per Capita Income: $800

Indigenous Population: 20%, primarily in rural lower class

Primary Exports:

Coffee	40%
Bauxite	25%
Cotton	10%
Other:	
Lumber	8%
Hemp	8%
Fruits	5%
Beef	4%

Imports from:

United States	50%
Japan	20%
West Germany	10%
Great Britain	10%
Latin America	5%
Others	5%

Principal Domestic Industry:

1. Food processing (including alcoholic beverages)
2. Textiles and clothing

Principal Foreign Industry:

1. American owned bauxite mining and smelting
2. Shell and Texaco oil refineries and retailers
3. Fiat automotive plant
4. Assorted chemicals and pharmaceuticals
5. Citibank and Bank of London
6. ITT-owned telephone and telegraph

Development Assistance Received 1945-1978:

U.S.: $40 million in grants; $150 million in loans; $50 million in MAP
World Bank: $90 million in loans for power plant, roads, ports

Government-Owned Enterprises:

1. All railroads
2. All electric power
3. Joint civilian-military managed steel plant
4. Industrial and agricultural investment banks

Major Political Events in San Mario History

1821—Independence from Spain.

1822—Chaos.

1826—Order restored under mestizo general, conservative upper class and Church.

1880—Anti-clerical Liberal Party takes power after short, bloody struggle; confiscates Church and Indian properties; encourages coffee planting and exports to U.S. and Europe.

1919—Anarchist and Socialist inspired labor unrest (primarily against foreign owned railways) leads to military coup and military rule.

1930—Military permits coalition of Liberal and Conservative parties to rule after a rigged election; invite foreign investment.

1938—Protesting students at USM organize clandestine Christian Democratic Party incorporating nationalistic and reform democratic ideologies; during 1940s they work among peasants and growing urban labor.

1956—Displeased with corruption in high places and growing student and labor protests, young officers lead a coup and nine months later hold country's first honest elections. Results: Christian Democrats—45%; Conservatives—20%; Socialists—14%; Communists—10%; Others—6%

Policy Consequences: Liberal labor laws; nationalization of railroads and electric power; new development bank; pass weak agrarian reform legislation but implement little; inflation increases from 10% in 1955 to 50% in 1961; balance of payments go from surplus to deficit.

1962—Military coup just before elections and military rule under General Carinoso.

Policy Consequences: Bauxite concessions granted on profit split of 60% to companies, 40% to government; foreign banks enter in larger numbers; extensive public works, including government steel plant; political parties intervened and communists jailed.

1972—Again dissatisfaction with corruption, growing protests, and now a small but vigorous guerrilla movement, military factions combine to remove Carinoso and promise to hold open elections within a year or two.

1975—Military decides to restore constitutional rule through free elections permitting all parties freedom to compete, then cancels elections one week before they were to be held.

1979—Military finally calls new elections.

Administration of the Latin America Simulation

1. Approximately six weeks before the exercise students will select the roles they will play by drawing from a hat. Between 12 and 20 roles can be used. When the number goes above 17 I just add a second peasant leader and labor leader and perhaps another political party.

2. During the weeks prior to the simulation the student is asked to prepare a six- to eight-page paper that describes the player he or she has selected and defines how they intend to play it. They are asked to do some library research on the player leading to their identification of its essential interests, allies and enemies as well as their likely positions on three or four typical issues selected by me. They must submit their papers to the instructor a couple of days before the simulation. The papers are not available to the players.

3. The students are given the names and phone numbers of all players as well as the rules of the game approximately two weeks before the simulation. They are encouraged to communicate with potential allies in an effort to develop coalitions.

4. The exercise occurs over two days, usually one three-hour session per day. It is important to adhere to the time limits listed in the rules for campaigns and other negotiations in order to get through at least four or five successive governments during the exercise.

The simulation is conducted within one large classroom with the players free to roam about discussing issues between votes. Order is restored for voting and votes are immediately collected by voice vote.

5. After the exercise has been completed, the students are asked to write a five-page paper analyzing its outcome. They are given three or four questions to guide them, focusing primarily on the perceived effects of several conditions on the outcome (as measured by the final point distribution); among them are: the original point distribution, coalition strategies followed, the postures assumed by critical players, the particular policies that were used to redistribute points. Their papers are discussed during a one-hour session.

6. Finally, one thing to remember: this is a zero-sum game; every policy must take points from a logical victim and redistribute them to a logical beneficiary. This becomes a major constraint on the design of policies and the maintenance of coalitions; nevertheless, it is used to emphasize the impact of scarcity on political behavior.

African Nation

Peter H. Koehn and Robert E. Eagle
University of Montana

1. *Subject Matter:* Domestic and international problems within selected African countries. Involves from two to five countries, depending upon the size of the class. Normally includes Nigeria, Tanzania, and Ethiopia.

2. *Courses and Levels for Which Simulation is Appropriate:* This simulation is appropriate for upper-division classes in African politics. The general structure of this simulation could be used in other comparative government classes.

3. *Number of Participants:* Minimum: 2 per country; Maximum: 12 per country; Optimum: 7-9 per country.

4. *Length of Time for Simulation:* 1 to 1½ hours for each country included.

5. *Schedule of Activities:* Students are given a problem by the instructor one class period prior to the actual simulation. The simulation consists of cabinet deliberations and decision-making, a public address made by the head of state, and occasionally, a referendum in which the entire class acts as the body politic. The cabinet session takes approximately 45 minutes to one hour, while the address by the head of state is completed in one to five minutes. A short discussion on the simulation takes place immediately following its conclusion.

6. *Required Physical Facilities:* One room, long table and movable chairs.

7. *Student Preparation for Simulation:* The instructor explains the nature of the simulation at one of the first classes at the beginning of the quarter. Students are allowed to select which country they would like to be part of. Approximately one to two hours of class time is devoted to group meetings of a preparatory nature. The instructor selects the roles to be played and students choose from among these. The instructor describes the library resources available as background material for the simulation and encourages the students to conduct a bibliographical search as the first part of their preparation for the simulation itself. Students are encouraged to divide the workload into research in books and parts of books found in the card catalog in the library, periodical literature as indexed by the Social Science Citation Index and the International Guide to Periodical Literature, as well as journals specifically devoted to African studies, current newspaper accounts found either in the library or in the State Department's Africa press clips, particularly valuable reference material such as Africa Confidential and the Africa Research Bulletin, and finally, materials found in the instructor's possession. Background research is absolutely essential to preparation for the simulation since most students involved in the class know very little about the African country that they play a role in. My observation is that the average student spends between 10 and 12 or 15 hours engaged in individual research in preparation for the simulation, and another five to ten hours in group preparation.

8. *Special Materials Needed:* Students use name tags to describe the role that they are playing during the simulation. Occasionally, students wear uniforms or other distinctive dress consistent with the roles that they are playing. No printed agenda is used as the format is simple enough to be explained orally.

9. *Other Features: Grading.* The grade the students receive for the simulation amounts to 20 percent of their total grade for the course. I've used varying methods for assigning grades and at present rely upon a system of peer evaluation whereby each participant receives a grade for his/her role in the simulation—50 percent of which comes from the individual grade that students in the class and involved in the simulation have assigned to that individual while the other 50 percent of the individual's grade is composed of the grade that the entire group receives for its performance as evaluated by the class as a whole, excluding the members of that group. I grade the students as well and my grade counts simply as one member of the class.

10. *Evaluation:* I have asked students enrolled in this class to evaluate the simulation in a standard student evaluation form along with other aspects of the class. In 1975, 51.7 percent of the class felt that the simulation was excellent as a learning device, 31 percent felt that it rated above average, and 6.9 percent felt that it was average, with 10 percent not responding. In 1976, 42 percent of the students felt that the simulation was an excellent learning device, 28 percent felt that it was above average, 3 percent rated it average, and 7 percent rated it poor. From my own observation, I would conclude that most students find the simulation to be an extremely interesting part of their learning experience in this class. This is evident from the amount of time that they put into preparation for the simulation and the enjoyment they seem to receive from the experience itself. In addition, some students have remarked to me on a later occasion that they found the simulation to be something that they remembered about the class and they found the problems it brought out to be very realistic in the context of contemporary African politics. In my opinion the simulation is an extremely valuable teaching device because it generates a high level of student enthusiasm and interest in learning which cannot be matched through simple lecturing. I firmly believe that the students attain much more knowledge about African politics by virtue of preparing for the simulation than they do by sitting through class lectures.

11. *Narrative:* The first step in the simulation is to divide the class into the number of countries that will be involved at a later date in discussing and deliberating over problems. Once students have been assigned to a particular group (that is, a specific country), they are given a list of roles that must be played during the course of the simulation. In all cases, the roles include the head of state and cabinet members who represent specific ministries or agencies. When appropriate, each ministry is designated with regard to whether or not its occupant is a civilian or military official. Students select roles within the first week or two of class. They are given five to six weeks to engage in research and preparation for the simulation.

One class period before the date of the simulation (that is at least two days in advance), the instructor presents a problem in domestic or international politics for the students to deal with in the simulation. The problem selected involves a major decision or, less frequently, a crisis of contemporary politics in that country. The problem is one of major political significance and ramifications to the country and is designed so that each member of the cabinet would be directly involved and affected by the outcome of the decision reached during the simulation. Students are informed that they must reach a decision of a positive or a negative character on the problem which they face.

There is some variation in what transpires during the actual simulation. In some cases an inner cabinet meets first to decide its position on the issue it faces. At the next stage the entire cabinet meets and, after some discussion that involves each member of the simulation taking a position of one sort or another on the issue on the agenda, a free-flowing discussion ensues, followed by a final decision. The head of state may choose to attend the cabinet meeting or send a representative to that meeting. As in most cabinet meetings, each member present is polled for his or her opinion on the issue at hand. However, the final decision is made by the head of state.

All inner-cabinet or full-cabinet sessions are held in front of the entire class (that is, those that are involved in simulations with other countries). Depending upon the outcome of the cabinet decision, the head of state may or may not elect to deliver an address to the nation which, in the context of the simulation, would involve a formal speech to the entire class. In some cases, I have found it appropriate to include a national referendum as the final stage of the simulation process. In such cases, each member of the class (including the role-playing participants for the country at issue) has one vote.

In discussing the simulation, I focus my comments on the degree to which students have played the roles which they selected in a realistic fashion. In addition, I attempt to suggest alternative lines of argumentation and reasoning which might have been utilized by participants in the simulation. Occasionally it might be necessary to correct a statement that was made during the course of simulation that was not factually accurate. Discussion of the simulation takes from five to 15 minutes.

Students are asked to grade the performance of the members of the simulation prior to the referendum if there is one. They are asked to grade students based not upon their own feelings with regard to the issue at hand, but with regard to the accuracy and comprehensiveness with which the participant represented his or her role. Students are given letter grades. It is important that the student evaluation be done at this time in order that neither the referendum nor the instructor's comments bias the results.

The Parliamentary Game

Louis E. Leopold
The Pennsylvania State University, Altoona Campus

Course/Level: Courses: Can be used in Comparative Government courses, especially Western Europe, as well as Introductory Political Science.

Level: The stress is on governance and leadership selection by party and/or coalition governments using parliamentary processes. Individual decision-making and bargaining are used to achieve personal, factional and party goals.

Number of Players: Very flexible. Simulation has run with as few as nine when French and German systems were being simulated at the same time, while 635 MPs actually play. Twenty to 30 seems ideal.

Roles (see sample chart for detail): Major Party Prime Minister, key cabinet and various MPs representing important factions and institutional influences (6-10 players). Major Opposition Party Leader, key Shadow Cabinet Members and major influencers (5-10 players). Major Third Party Leader, Rivals, MPs, Youth Leader (1-5 players). Other opposition parties (1).

Timing: One week. In Comparative Western courses role playing may be continued to examine various aspects of the course, including comparisons with mini-German (Federal Republic) and French Game Teams. This may be particularly useful in illustrating European Community relationships.

Stages:
1. Briefing on the "State of the Parties" after an election in which the government has come in first but without achieving an overall majority. An invitation from Buckingham Palace to form a new government.
2. Bargaining and negotiations within and between the parties in an effort to form a government.
3. Forming the government; gaining the confidence of Parliament!
4. Governance-maintaining confidence and power while dealing with a set of issues.

Physical Facilities: Minimum: One sizeable classroom with separate caucus areas. Preferred: Separate rooms for major party caucus and for private negotiations.

Preparation: Can vary with course. With Comparative—Western Europe, the simulation may follow materials on parties and elections and act as a bridge to governing. Course readings on parliamentary government structure may be assigned simultaneously with the play. A briefing sheet on the overall election campaign, including the key events and issues, should be handed out to supplement the oral briefing. Oral briefings can be presented as BBC reports, videotaped if desired.

Special Materials:
1. Sketch of roles. These may be fictionalized versions based in part on real world players. Some may prefer to use major players directly from the current scene and to encourage library research to complete details.
2. Negotiation forms for government makeup and support, including issues and personnel appointments.
3. Identification tags, giving role and party.
4. Major issues briefing packet—the key issues with which the government must deal.
5. Debriefing form—self analysis of relation between role playing actions and interests, by stages.

Narrative: After the briefing on the "State of the Parties" the leader of the party with the largest number of seats is invited by the Queen to form a government. Only the leader may *authorize* negotiations with the leaders of other parties for official support. Negotiated understandings must be ratified by a majority of the party (based on influence points held by each role player)*, representing differing party factions. After negotiations are completed, the leader submits his proposed new government to Parliament for approval—which requires a plurality

---

*See Sample Chart.

Sample 24-Player Chart

Group Roles	Votes/ Influence Points	Group Roles	Votes/ Influence Points
Labour and Allies	46	Conservative and Unionists	44
Party Leader, Prime Minister	9	Party Leader	9
Parliament Private Secretary to PM	1	Deputy Leader	3
Leader—Wedgwood Left Wing	3	Far Right Leader	5
Leader—Trade Union Congress	8	Ex-Leader	5
Leader—Tribune Left Wing	4	Progressive Wing Leader	7
Loyal Back Bench Spokesperson (England)	10	Loyal Back Bench Spokesperson (England)	10
Back Bench Spokesperson (Scotland)	2	Loyal Back Bench Spokesperson (Scotland)	2
Social Democracy Moderate Leader	4	Young Conservative Leader	1
Social Democracy Activist Leader	4	Ulster Unionist *Dissident* Leader	2
Young Socialist Leader	1	Scottish Nationalist Party	3
		Party Leader	3
Liberal Party	7		
Party Leader	3		
Challenger	1		
Scottish Liberal Leader	2		
Young Liberal Leader	1		

of Parliament's influence points. If the leader fails to submit or is unable to win parliamentary support within the specified time limit, the opposition leader is invited to attempt to form a government.

In the round after a government is formed, the government selects three issues from the issue packet and must submit its recommendations to Parliament on these for approval. Issues can be chosen to cover key course topics (i.e., Home Rule for Scotland, Ireland, abolition of the House of Lords, nationalization of insurance, relations with the European Community, a Wealth Tax, Labour Management or Productivity, Foreign Policy). The government falls if a vote of no confidence is adopted by Parliament.

Further sessions may be scheduled to illustrate basic systems aspects during the balance of the course. For comparative purposes an interesting option has been to convert the British team at this point to eight to ten essential roles, while the other students form comparable German and French groups. Throughout, they attempt to deal with European Community problems, with one or more students playing European Community roles. When using this option, the simulation may be operated for 30 minutes or more weekly for the balance of the course. In addition to the usual debriefing, examination essay questions may focus on the assigned role playing perspectives.

Some may prefer to have roles, parliamentary power distribution and major issue concerns reflect real time circumstances as far as is practicable. This permits flexibility in focus on different constraints. Party influence point scores can be adjusted accordingly. Major role players may be constrained against cooperation under specific circumstances.

Forging Economic Development Policy in Third World Countries*

JoAnn F. Aviel
San Francisco State University

The primary objective of this simulation was to stimulate interest in and improve perception of the complex processes by which leaders of Third World countries make specific policy decisions to develop their national economies. The simulation was originally written by Don Barnhart in Social Sciences and myself in International Relations as part of an introductory experimental course in Latin American Area Studies. It has since been successfully adapted for classes at all college levels dealing with foreign policy and development questions. The simulation is based on a recent factual situation in a Third World country which is called "Alpha." At that time a major question of public policy was how to reorganize the automobile industry to stimulate national economic development. Although the government had the responsibility for deciding basic policies, agreement on specific details as well as effective implementation depended upon generating support from many different groups in various parts of the country.

To dramatize the issues and policy alternatives, the participants are initially divided into four groups. The Governmental Group represents the military officers who succeeded in overthrowing an ineffective civilian government and launched an intense propaganda campaign to convince the citizenry that the new government would move decisively to free the country from the evils of international dependency and domestic poverty. The Capitolia Group represents the dominant political and economic interests of the country. The Provincia Group, living in a relatively impoverished and tradition-bound provincial capital 500 miles into the interior, seeks an effective decentralization of economic and political power from the national capital to the provinces. Finally, a Common Market Group represents the interests of the five-nation Common Market, whose members have agreed on paper to a high degree of international economic cooperation and development planning. Each participant is assigned a specific

---

*A full description of this simulation and optional exercises together with the materials distributed to students is scheduled to be published by Gerald Thorpe of Indiana University of Pennsylvania, editor, Consortium for International Studies Education (CISE), Occasional Paper Series.

role and given a brief description of who the person is, and what her/his primary objectives and goals are in the simulation, but with the freedom to expand and elaborate on these given characteristics. Twenty-four roles have been designed: the Governmental Group consists of the President and Ministers of Agriculture, Industry, Economy, and Labor; the Capitolia Group includes a newspaper reporter, professor of economics, labor representative, leader of the Organization of the Unemployed, head of the Chamber of Commerce, the Archbishop, and the managers of the Chrysler, Ford, and Toyota Motor Company plants; the Provincia Group includes a newspaper reporter, professor of economics, head of the Chamber of Commerce, labor representative, and leader of the Organization of the Unemployed; and the Diplomatic Group consists of the Ministers of the Economy from Beta, Carla, Delta, and Edna, together with the United States Ambassador. Roles can be expanded by adding more government officials, labor representatives, and unemployed. The number of roles can be reduced by eliminating the diplomatic group and/or additional roles from each of the other groups.

The actual role-playing activities require a minimum of two classroom hours. Preliminary and follow-up activities can vary according to the needs of the instructor and class. A brief description of the minimum suggested activities follows. At the first session students receive an assignment to one particular role with students usually volunteering for specific roles. Three short simulated newspaper articles are distributed which present the substantive facts and issues upon which the simulation is based, including a description of the initial government decision to reorganize the automobile industry. Directions are given for preparing preliminary position papers and final evaluation papers. The preliminary paper consists of answers to a series of questions calling for participants to define their interests, goals, and alternatives regarding the government degree and to prepare their strategy by analyzing who would be their probable allies and opponents and the actions they could take to achieve their goals. Although students can be assigned additional reading appropriate to their role, the position paper can be prepared on the basis of the three articles distributed, which total only seven pages. The position paper is to be handed in before beginning the simulation. Students are instructed to keep a copy for themselves and to keep their responses secret from some of those playing other roles since the decision-making process involves some degree of secrecy, surprise, and impromptu innovation and reaction.

The simulation itself is divided into two principal phases. Phase I begins with the four different groups physically separated from each other in separate rooms if possible. This phase ends with the Governmental Group announcing the details of its Final Decree after considering all its options. Members of the other groups are instructed to implement the strategies to achieve their objectives as sketched out in their individual position papers. This includes reaching decisions appropriate to each interest and each regional group concerning their reactions to the announced terms of the Final Decree and influencing members of the Governmental Group concerning the specific terms of the Decree. Communication between individuals in different groups may be accomplished by travel between Capitolia, Provincia and the sister republics by any one who may reasonably be expected to be able to do so, publication of appropriate "newscasts" by the reporters, and by mailing written requests for information, interviews, or meetings with the instructor delivering such requests to the designated person.

In Phase II each participant and/or group of participants must decide what their reaction is to the Final Decree of the Government with the goal of taking some specific action(s) to support, modify, or reject its implementation. This phase is normally briefer than the previous one. The instructor can either set a definite time to terminate this phase at the beginning, or vary the time according to the extent of interest and motivation which is perceived on the part of the participants.

After the simulation has terminated students are instructed to prepare a brief evaluation paper for discussion at the following debriefing session. In the paper and accompanying discussion students are asked which goals they achieved and why, and which they failed to achieve and why. They are asked whether their original interpretation of their interests, allies, opponents, and strategy changed during the simulation and the reasons for change or lack of change. They are asked to evaluate their own feelings about their role and the roles played by others. Their evaluation of the problem of economic development is assessed through questions such as the following:

Why is it so difficult for countries to reach a consensus about economic development policies?

Why are Third World countries considered to be dependent and why is it difficult for them to break their bonds of dependency?

Why do so many developing countries abandon a democratic decision-making process in favor of a more authoritarian process?

What do you feel to be some of the most important problems and processes of economic development?

Finally students are asked what they liked best and what least about participating in the simulation and how could the simulation be changed so as to make it a better learning experience.

The response of students to the simulation has been quite positive. Even when they found parts of the process frustrating, they usually felt they had learned more about the problems of decision-making than they could through the more traditional methods of lectures or readings.

A number of optional follow-up exercises were designed which adapt the simulation to the level of student preparation and the length of time the instructor wishes to devote to this topic. Maps were used to describe the location of industries and production patterns in the United States and world-wide. A list of case studies dealing with the transport industry was compiled and students were asked to compare the simulation results to one or more case studies. Students could choose to analyze data generated by the simulation or case studies to test propositions about bargaining and negotiation in general or with respect to the making of economic policy in developing countries. Students could also write position papers regarding the establishment of a selected industry in a real world country by assuming the role of director of economic planning or of United States or United Nations consultants hired by the country. While these optional exercises expand the learning experience provided by the simulation, they are not necessary and students have applied lessons learned in the simulation to subsequent assignments in a variety of ways.

The Geneva Conference on the Middle East

Lewis Brownstein
State University of New York, College at New Paltz

I. Overview

Subject Matter: Simulates a conference at which participants attempt to negotiate a single agenda (e.g., future of the West Bank and Gaza Strip) related to the Arab-Israel conflict.

Course and Levels: Can be used in courses on international politics of the Middle East, Israel in World Politics, the Arab-Israel conflict. Can also be modified for use in other international relations courses. The format can be used to simulate any multilateral international conference.

Maximum and Minimum Number of Players: There are eight roles allowing for a maximum of 16 players (two to a team): United States, Soviet Union, Israel, Syria, Jordan, Egypt, Palestinians, United Nations. Since the United Nations could be optional, game could be run with as few as seven.

Length of Time: Minimum—three hours (exclusive of debriefing); Maximum—open-ended; Recommended—four hours.

Periods: Conference alternates 20 minutes on and 20 minutes off. While in session, there are procedures for public negotiation. When the conference is in recess, delegations have an opportunity for private bargaining. (See below for specifics on procedures for conference.)

Minimum Physical Facilities: One large room with large conference table or moveable seats which can be placed in a circle and at least one additional room or adjacent hallway where private negotiations can occur. If possible, it would be desirable to have a number of rooms available for private contacts but this has not been essential.

Preparation: Students must prepare by reading fairly extensively on the history, political systems and negotiation positions of their respective states. In addition, they need some familiarity with the positions of the other participants as well as the key negotiating resolutions of the United Nations (Resolutions 242 and 338). The greater the preparation, the more sophisticated the negotiations which occur. Once the confidential instructions are passed out, each team must plan its strategy for the conference. This requires at least one and preferably two meetings with the instructor to be certain everyone understands the issues and is prepared to negotiate them. In all, preparation time required will be at least three to four weeks.

Special Materials: Each team should prepare name tags to be worn during the simulation, country name plates and flags to be placed before the delegation while the conference is in session. There should be a large-sized map of Israel and the occupied territories available for reference. Delegations will require note-pads and writing materials for framing resolutions during the simulation. A blackboard will be needed to write out the resolutions being considered by the conference at any one time.

Experience: Each time this simulation has been run, students have been enthusiastic about the experience. They have generally worked quite hard preparing it and have seemed to learn a great deal from participating in it. The only problems which have arisen resulted from lack of preparation on the part of some participants or unforeseen contingencies (e.g., sickness).

II. Detailed Description

Goals: This simulation has three overall learning goals.

(1) It attempts to motivate students to examine intensively the issues in the Arab-Israel conflict from the perspective of one of the participants. In preparing for the conference students research the issues extensively. Since they do this with a particular goal in mind, they are able to define the specific information they require with the expectation that they will be making practical use of it. Students participating in this acquire sophisticated and detailed background on the political, economic, social and geopolitical factors in the conflict.

(2) The simulation gives students some appreciation for the difficulties of multilateral negotiations in an international system. They have to grapple with such problems as: how to build a viable coalition of support for a particular position; how to bargain with a variety of states simultaneously; and how to operate with the constraints imposed by domestic political pressures, alliance politics, and differentials in power.

(3) Students learn some of the procedures for operating in a formal meeting. They learn to frame precise written motions; to amend, debate and vote on them. Use of Robert's Rules of Order gives them some familiarity with those procedures.

Grading: The students are graded on preparation only, not on their performance in the actual simulation. There are two reasons for this: (1) The emphasis is thereby placed on careful preparation; (2) once the simulation begins, it is not possible for the instructor to follow everything which happens since much of the action occurs in private negotiating sessions.

Preparation for the Simulation: Preparation by the instructor is essential for the success of the exercise. Students must know what is expected of them, how they can most expeditiously acquire the information they require, and how much time they will need for preparation. Preparation can be divided into three phases:

(1) *Selection of participants:* The procedure used has been self-selection. Students are not required to participate since some find it threatening. Each student chooses which team he wishes to join. They must hand in first, second, and third choices in case too many want the same team. Since the simulation takes time to prepare, students are told that once they commit themselves it is understood they will not drop the course. Since unforeseen contingencies can arise (sickness, failure to prepare) it is best to have two people per team so that there is a reasonable certainty that all teams will be represented.

(2) *Preliminary research:* At the first meeting students are given a list of basic bibliographic sources and texts on the Middle East to get them started on their research. They are instructed to gather background on their states: history, economy, leadership, and policies in the Arab-Israel conflict with particular reference to the issues to be dealt with at Geneva. They are required to bring themselves up to date on their country's policies in the area since they will have to reflect them at the conference. They are counseled to examine, as much as possible, the respective positions of the other participants as well. This preliminary research should take about three weeks. Before proceeding to the next phase, meetings are held with each team to evaluate the quality of their preparation thus far.

(3) *Preparation on the agenda item:* One week before the actual simulation all teams are given the agenda item, copies of the procedures for the conference, and their respective confidential negotiating instructions. It is best to wait until this point to reveal the subject of negotiation so as to encourage students to take an overall perspective in examining their states' foreign policy goals during the initial research phase. Teams are instructed to spend the next week preparing a negotiating strategy for the conference: i.e., maximum and minimum goals, prospective coalition partners, anticipated competing coalitions, and so on. Strong emphasis is placed on the necessity of staying within the guidelines of the confidential instructions. Just prior to the conference the instructor meets one last time with each team. At that time, they discuss how and what the team has prepared, what they anticipate will happen and any matters the students may wish to raise. If they have not worked it out on their own, the instructor may wish to separately apprise each team of the range of possible or feasible outcomes. For example, in negotiating the future of the West Bank and Gaza the outcomes included an independent Palestinian state, confederation of the

territories with Jordan or Israel, federation with Jordan or Israel, autonomous region linked to both Jordan and Israel, unitary Jordanian state, annexation by Israel. The distinction between political and security issues should also be clarified. Finally, the instructor should meet with all teams together in order to review conference procedures. This should include such things as: how to offer resolutions; how to amend resolutions on the floor; and voting procedures.

(4) *Confidential negotiating instructions:* The instructor will have to write confidential negotiating instructions for each delegation. The specifics of the instructions will vary according to what is on the agenda. In general, however, instructions should be designed to set limits on the delegations, leaving leeway for them to negotiate with each other over specifics. Thus, each set of instructions should focus on prohibitions rather than attempt to impose a specific negotiating strategy. Delegations should also be restricted in terms of the specific alliances they can form. Thus, the Israelis were instructed to oppose an independent state on the West Bank under all circumstances and not to break with the United States irrevocably. The aim of the instructions should be to place realistic restrictions on the participants while leaving room for substantive negotiations to occur; to avoid unrealistic agreements without predetermining the outcome.

Procedures: The full list of conference procedures is appended to this description. This section will briefly discuss the rationale for some of them.

Number 1: The conference has a time limit as a means of putting pressure on the participants to reach an agreement. It could be run without one.

Number 3: The UN representative chairs as a compensation for a low voting weight.

Number 4: It was found in an earlier version that permitting communication *between* delegations during the conference was disruptive.

Number 7: Requiring all resolutions in writing makes for an orderly procedure and forces precision on the participants.

Number 8: The voting weights are designed to force coalition-building. Requiring a two-thirds vote to pass, necessitates extensive negotiations. Instructors may wish to alter the weights as they plan their own simulations.

Number 9: The instructor acts as the referee. It is the responsibility of the referee to see to it that no delegation violates its instructions. The referee must also write out the resolutions being considered on the blackboard, time the debate, and tally the votes.

Number 13: The conference is restricted to the agenda item in order to prevent extraneous issues from arising. Delegations may, however, negotiate other issues in the private sessions and should be encouraged to do so if this is a means of reaching agreement on the issue being dealt with at the conference. It is at this point that the prior preparation and research pays off.

Debriefing: Experience has shown that debriefing should occur immediately after the conference is over, while memories are fresh and enthusiasm high. Questions might deal with such things as:

1. What happened in the private discussions
2. Problems with the procedures
3. Ambiguity in the instructions
4. Value of the experience

This is a very important phase since it enables the instructor to identify the problem areas in design and execution with a view to revisions.

Procedures for the Conference

Agenda: The Future of the West Bank and Gaza

Place and Time: FT 504, 5 PM sharp on December 7, 1977

1. The conference will last for three hours after which there will be a one-half hour debriefing.
2. The conference will run for 20 minutes on and 20 minutes off.
3. The conference will be chaired by the UN representative. Only those recognized by the Chair may speak.
4. No notes or other communications may be passed *between* delegations while the conference is in session.
5. While the conference is in session, only one member of the delegation may speak for that delegation. Members will alternate between sessions.
6. Consultations may take place within delegations while the conference is in session.
7. All formal proposals or resolutions to be presented to the conference must be put in writing. Amendments may be offered to any motion on the floor.
8. All decisions at the conference, whether on amendments or main motions, must be reached by *two-thirds majority* of those present and voting (except see number 12). Votes are distributed as follows:

United States	20
Soviet Union	20
Egypt	15
Israel	15
Syria	15
Jordan	10
United Nations	5
Palestinians	10
TOTAL	110

9. Any doubts which a delegation may have concerning its instructions should be referred to the referee.
10. The conference will begin with each delegation making an opening statement in which it presents its proposal for a settlement and gives its justification for it. These will be three-minute statements only and should be

detailed. From then on, any main proposal on the floor must be voted on within 20 minutes of its being made except that amendments to it will take precedence and must be voted on within five minutes of being made.

11. If no settlement is reached, the conference will be deemed a failure with war the probable outcome.

12. Any delegation may walk out at any time. In order to return, it will have to be accepted by a vote of the majority of the remaining delegations according to the weighted system. The withdrawal of any four delegations will result in an immediate termination of the conference and its consequent failure.

13. Only the agenda item may be negotiated in the open session. No other items can be dealt with or raised. Any delegation raising extraneous issues will be ruled out of order by the chair. Agreements can only be reached in the conference.

Confidential Instructions: United States

A. Our goal is a settlement acceptable to all parties. If possible, we would like to minimize the Soviet role. Excluding them is probably unrealistic. We must attempt to play a mediating role. We remain fairly flexible as to the final shape of an agreement but certain things are firm:

1. Under no circumstances must we agree to the presence of Soviet troops in the area in a peacekeeping capacity.

2. Israel's fundamental security interests must be protected.

3. U.S. troops should likewise not be used nor should we agree to a mutual defense pact with any of the parties unless this single point stands in the way of an agreement.

4. We must not permit the conference to break down.

5. We must avoid being tied to one or the other. Ours is a mediating role.

B. As to the West Bank itself:

1. Israel will have to give it up. We must be firm on this point.

2. We would prefer to see it returned to Jordanian control with some provision for local autonomy and demilitarization but we could accept a Palestinian state.

3. The Allon plan would be acceptable.

4. If it proves impossible to get acceptance of a Jordanian control, we are prepared to accept the establishment of a Palestinian state with these provisos:

   a. it must be demilitarized
   b. it would be restricted to the West Bank and Gaza with some form of corridor under Israeli control.

5. It may become necessary to apply substantial pressure to Israel at some point to get a settlement. This should be avoided, if possible, but not at the risk of a settlement and the success of the conference itself.

6. Any Israeli withdrawal must be accompanied by an Arab statement recognizing explicitly Israel's legitimacy.

Confidential Instructions: Soviet Union

A. Our goal is to break the U.S. diplomatic monopoly in the Middle East and by the shape of the agreement to make it clear that we cannot be excluded.

B. We are anxious to see a settlement but not at the risk of our relations with Syria and the Palestinians.

C. We support the establishment of a Palestinian state in the West Bank and Gaza. As elements of a settlement we hold the following positions:
1. We are prepared to participate in a peacekeeping force along with the U.S.
2. We oppose demilitarization but will accept it if the Arabs agree.
3. Under no circumstances must Israel be permitted to keep the territories.
4. The Allon plan is not acceptable, but we might accept some minor border changes.

D. We must avoid a split with the leading Arab states Egypt and Syria. We may have to break with one, but not with both.

E. We must insist on the legitimacy of the Palestinians' claims and represent their positions wherever possible. If a settlement seems possible, we should encourage the Palestinians to accept it rather than see the conference fail.

Confidential Instructions: Egypt

A. Our goals at the conference are:
1. A settlement. This is a vital interest. The conference must not fail.
2. Recognition of Egypt's leadership position in the Arab world.
3. Avoidance of diplomatic isolation. We cannot remain isolated from both Syria and Jordan.
4. Israeli withdrawal from the West Bank and Gaza.
5. Establishment of a Palestinian state.
6. Failing number 5, we are prepared to see the establishment of a federated state with Jordan providing for local autonomy.
7. To keep the U.S. engaged in the area and to keep the Soviet Union as much as possible on the sidelines.

B. We oppose:
1. Demilitarization of the West Bank and Gaza.
2. The Allon Plan. We insist on total withdrawal with perhaps minor changes.

C. We could support:
  1. A UN force without superpower participation.
  2. A limited forces agreement.

Confidential Instructions: Israel

A. Our goal at the Conference is to avoid giving up the territories if at all possible.
  1. A stalemate at the conference would be acceptable *but only if we are not blamed for it.* We can walk out only if we do it along with others.

B. If it should prove necessary to give up the territories we could accept a return of the West Bank to Jordan if:
  1. The Allon plan is implemented combined perhaps with some form of confederated state.
  2. The West Bank is demilitarized.
  3. The Arab states explicitly accept our right to exist.
  4. Any corridor to Gaza is under our control.
  5. We receive guarantees from the United States for our security.

C. Under no circumstances are we prepared to see the establishment of a Palestinian state on the West Bank.

D. We must aim at direct negotiations with the Arabs whenever possible.

E. We must resist any attempt by the Soviet Union to play a direct role in the implementation of a settlement in the area. Especially we oppose the presence of Soviet troops in the area.

F. We will not negotiate with the PLO or recognize it in any way. This does not prevent us from negotiation with other groups of Palestinians.

Confidential Instructions: Syria

A. Our goals at the Conference are:
  1. Establishment of a Palestinian state in the West Bank and Gaza.
  2. Failing number 1, we could accept Palestinian confederation with Jordan but only if the Palestinians themselves agreed to it.
  3. Acceptance of the principle of total withdrawal by Israel.
  4. Avoidance of diplomatic isolation.
  5. Avoidance of a conference breakdown but we will leave rather than acquiesce to Israeli control.
  6. We must not break with both Egypt or Jordan although we could accept a breach with one of them.

B. We oppose:
   1. Demilitarization.
   2. The Allon Plan in any form.

C. We could support:
   1. An international force so long as it was on both sides of the border but not with superpower participation.

D. We will not talk directly to the Israelis. We must insist on the use of a mediator.

E. Under no circumstances can we be held responsible for a failure to achieve a Palestinian state.

Confidential Instructions: Jordan

A. Our goals at the conference are:
   1. To regain control of the West Bank if at all possible. This could take the form of a federation with local autonomy.
   2. Failing that, we could support a demilitarized Palestinian state. In this case, our goal would be to keep it either allied with us or out of all alliances.
   3. We must avoid diplomatic isolation especially from the United States, Syria or Egypt. Under no circumstances can we break with all of these states. We could accept a schism with one if other vital interests are at stake.
   4. Given 1-3, we are anxious for a settlement but we could accept the status quo.

B. On specifics:
   1. We could support the Allon Plan especially if this meant getting the West Bank back.
   2. We oppose demilitarization if we can get control but we could accept it.
   a. we would prefer a UN force to demilitarization
   b. we would strongly oppose the presence of Russian troops in such a force.

   3. We would rather not see a Palestinian state but we will accept it rather than be diplomatically isolated from Egypt and Syria.

C. We will avoid negotiating directly with the Israelis in public. We will insist on a mediator for any public exchanges.

Confidential Instructions: United Nations

Our goal is to see a settlement acceptable to all sides in which we play a role in facilitating and implementing an agreement.
   1. We believe the *status quo* is not viable.
   a. Israel must withdraw in order for peace to be possible.

b. some public acceptance of Israel by the Arabs is probably necessary.

2. We must strive not to be frozen out of the negotiations.

a. This means we cannot alienate any significant party.

3. An ideal outcome would be if all sides turned to us to mediate the settlement.

4. Whatever the settlement, we must push for the retention of the UN force to monitor the settlement, preferably without superpower participation.

Confidential Instructions: Palestinians

A. Our goals are:
1. Establishment of a state under our rule in the West Bank and Gaza.
2. Avoidance of direct recognition of Israel. We must remain vague on this.
3. Strengthening of the Soviet role in the negotiations.
4. Avoidance of diplomatic isolation from Egypt and Syria. On account can we break with both of these states.

B. We oppose:
1. Demilitarization of the West Bank and Gaza.
2. U.S. participation in a peacekeeping force.
3. Anything less than full sovereignty.

C. We will not speak nor negotiate with Israel directly.

World Security and Disarmament Conference

Ralph M. Goldman
San Francisco State University

The instructional objective of the course on "Arms Control and Peacekeeping" was to provide an historical, technological, and political introduction to the relationships among national and global security, the arms race, and international peacekeeping. The simulation, which comfortably incorporates from 12 to 20 students, represented the work of a preparatory commission for a World Security and Disarmament Conference. The task of the Preparatory Commission was to design an agenda for the world conference and to prepare a working draft of a world security and disarmament treaty or body of resolutions.

Each student was required to select a country whose delegate he or she would become during the simulation. The roster of countries on the Preparatory Commission was designed to provide a broad representation of nuclear, nonnuclear, developed, developing, and regionally significant nations. These included: Algeria, Brazil, Canada, Egypt, France, India, Iran, Israel, Japan,

Malaysia, Nigeria, People's Republic of China, Sri Lanka, Sweden, Soviet Union, United Kingdom, United States, Venezuela, West Germany, and Yugoslavia.

In order to assure that well-diversified background knowledge would find its way into the simulation, each student was required to specialize in (a) some arms control topic such as deterrence, nuclear theft, conventional weapons, strategic weapons, inspection, test ban, qualitative controls, etc., and (b) a particular peacekeeping topic such as the Uniting-for-Peace Resolution, the United Nations Emergency Force, collective security, or one of the many peacekeeping missions. Each student wrote a 1,000-word background paper on his or her topics for distribution to the other members of the class. Each student also prepared a brief opening statement to be delivered to the Commission describing his or her nation's expectations. The major preparatory requirement was a substantial *National Strategy Memorandum,* a secret set of instructions to the delegate from the leaders of his or her government reminding the delegate of (a) relevant historical, geographical, economic, and political conditions impinging upon the nation's foreign policy, (b) pertinent domestic political considerations that might relate to the work of a World Security and Disarmament Conference, and (c) the security, arms control, disarmament, and peacekeeping policy postures of the nation during the past decade.

The instructor provided real-world background by distributing to the class Chapter II of *The United Nations and Disarmament, 1970-1975,* a report of the Department of Political and Security Council Affairs of the United Nations. This chapter describes recent United Nations efforts to convene a World Disarmament Conference. More recent runs of the simulation have included references to recent reports by The Stanley Foundation of Muscatine, Iowa, anticipating the UN Special Session on Disarmament to be convened in 1978.[1]

The simulated meetings of the Preparatory Commission were conducted during seven 3½-hour class sessions. After a great deal of realistic haggling over the selection of Commission officers and the adoption of Commission procedures, the class devolved into six drafting subcommittees dealing with the following topics: nuclear weapons; regional treaties; inspection and enforcement; conventional weapons; economic aspect of disarmament; and monitoring the implementation of the treaty. For classes unable to devote seven sessions to the simulation, it is possible to accomplish a great deal of realism and experience in three or four sessions focusing on one or two sections of a treaty draft.

Each subcommittee agreed to follow the same general outline in its drafting work: a statement of the problem with which it would be dealing; enumeration of guidelines and principles for resolution of these problems; recommended specific treaty provisions, and specification of any unfinished business that would have to be pursued in the future. Each subcommittee was to reveal its points of disagreement by using brackets or underscoring for sentences, phrases,

---

[1] *UN Special Session on Disarmament,* Report of the Eighth Annual Conference on United Nations Procedures, May 5-8, 1977, and *Multilateral Disarmament and the Special Session,* Report of the Twentieth Conference on the United Nations of the Next Decade, June 19-25, 1977.

or words in dispute. The final working draft of the treaty (or body of resolutions) to be presented to the full world conference used the same procedure for bracketing or underscoring disputed terminology or guidelines. The simulation actually produced a 19-page draft treaty which was surprisingly innovative in some respects and clearly pointed up, through bracketing and underscoring, expected points of disagreement likely to be found in the real world, e.g., the definition of a "conventional weapon."

The only physical requirement for the simulation was a seminar room with a conference or seminar table or tables. The room was large enough to permit subcommittee meetings in different parts of the room. An optional piece of equipment was a tape recorder to make a permanent record of the proceedings. The tape was also useful to the Preparatory Commission secretary responsible for preparing minutes of each full Commission session.

The instructor assumed the roles of God, Devil, and Nature. This permitted him to confer privately with individual delegates (God), introduce issues into the Commission proceedings through the mouths of different delegates (Devil), and, from time to time, evaluate the day's session by pointing to the remarkable similarities between the classroom simulation and the realities of international politics (Nature).

Typically, most students adopted the roles, attitudes, and political strategies that could be expected of their respective nations. The instructor and the students were repeatedly reminded of and impressed by how much of the "real-world" was coming into the classroom. For example, at the height of the civil war in Angola, the issue of the legitimacy of the Angolan representative tied up proceedings for several hours. As might be expected, the better prepared the student, the more fully he or she executed the appropriate role behavior of his or her nation. In at least one simulation, a Third World coalition emerged which was skillfully outmanuvered by a First World coalition on several procedural matters. National interests and strategies became evident during the reading and debates over the subcommittee treaty drafts. The debates, it should be noted, required a relatively strong and skillful chairperson; in one instance, this was the Swedish delegate. The students soon realized that not all delegates were peace-loving or concerned with world institutional development and that domestic political considerations and global propaganda objectives were significant motivations.

Student involvement and morale was high throughout the simulation, which took place during the later half of the semester. The "final examination" consisted of the concluding session of the Preparatory Commission, during which final drafting details and unresolved disputes were recorded. This final session concluded with a dinner celebration at the instructor's home. Copies of the final treaty draft were subsequently typed and mailed to each student as a memento of the experience and a record of the substantive discussions.[2]

---

[2] A full report of this simulation may be found in John H. Sloane, Ralph M. Goldman, and Paul Magnelia, *Simulation of Global Politics; Some Classroom Experiences in the California System* (School of Behavioral and Social Sciences, San Francisco State University, 1976).

World Disarmament Conference

Seth Thompson
Loyola Marymount University

I

Subject: The simulation focuses on two basic phenomena: foreign policy formation from a bureaucratic politics perspective and negotiations over arms control or disarmament.

Courses: Designed for junior or senior level courses in International Politics, International Organization, or foreign policy; has been used in a freshman level introductory course.

Players: There are nine distinct roles in the simulation: controllers and defenders in each of four hypothetical nations and a Director's role that includes a press function as well as responsibility for overall administration (normally filled by a faculty member). Eight players is the minimum for the simulation (a smaller version can be created by deleting the two smaller nations, Cobo and Matro, and focusing on bilateral interactions); there is no absolute maximum but it is probably unwise to use more than 32 players. Each role (except Director) is designed to be played as a group. There is no necessity for the groups to be of similar size; it may be desirable to have slightly larger groups representing Yolo and Zeno.

Time: Can be run in a minimum of two class sessions plus time for debriefing; five class sessions is probably the maximum feasible. The actual conference period can be relatively open-ended depending on progress of bargaining.

Periods: (1) Group playing each role meets separately to formulate position on national policy (approximately 30 minutes); (2) Controllers and defenders within each nation meet to formulate national policy and composition of negotiating team (minimum 30-40 minutes); (3) Negotiators from four nations meet in conference to discuss arms issues; (4) (optional) Nations meet separately to ratify agreement, if reached. Decision rules within each nation at the discretion of Director (maximum 30 minutes).

Facilities: No special requirements, beyond a room large enough to permit eight initial meetings and a central area for the conference itself.

Materials: No special materials needed; participants should be encouraged to develop documentation for conference sessions.

II

This simulation re-creates some of the dynamics surrounding arms control problems and negotiations in the recent past. There are two distinct phases of the simulation, the first reflecting processes at the national level and the second focusing on systems level of international dynamics.

The game is loosely structured, in the sense that there is no dominant solution and participants may end up with a four-party agreement, a two-party private deal, or no agreement at all. The environment is passive since there are no other actors providing input to the simulation, although the Director may wish to simulate other actors if needed.

During the first phase, participants should be discouraged from face to face communication with players in other countries. Initially, communication should be limited to members of the same sub-group with each nation (e.g., Yolo's controllers should devote their attention to formulating their own position). The press function is always available to the players and can be handled by submitting an item to the Director who will then announce it publicly, with some indication of whether the item is an official government statement (only available to controllers), an "informed source," or a rumor.

Although the four nations represented in the simulation are closely modeled on real world analogues, it is not necessary for participants to identify Yolo as the USSR, Zeno as the U.S., Matro as China, or Cobo as any one of several near-nuclear states. The simulation permits participants to add new elements, such as conventional forces of forward based systems, within the constraints of plausibility, although they ought to be discouraged from doing so. The issue of the "Laser Missile Defense" allows the exploration of the dynamics of escalation and the consequences of developing "bargaining chips." In part, the richness of the game relies on the sophistication of the players but there is no necessity for players with extensive background in arms control questions or familiarity with current positions and policies. The game can be an effective teacher of players with an overly simple approach to arms questions.

The decision to move the simulation from one phase or period to another rests with the Director and his/her judgment that players have completed one set of tasks. This is normally clear from the context. Although not necessary, it is highly desirable to have at least one natural break during the third phase of the simulation to permit consultation and/or quiet negotiations among nations.

III

Issues for Debriefing: Debriefing sessions might focus on some or all of the following major issues:

Differences in perceptions and issues among groups within the same country

Differences in approach to arms questions between countries with different kinds of arsenals and international status

Use of press function to communicate bargaining positions and intentions or confuse issues

Extent to which presence of smaller states facilitated or hindered agreement

Timing and consequences of concessions

It may be helpful to stress in the debriefing that the simulation is not "rigged" to produce a specific outcome; some past runs have ended up with consensual agreements, some have ended up with two-party agreements, and some have ended up with no agreement at all.

IV

Players' Materials

Introduction

Men and women who have dreamed of a world without war have often come to believe that abolishing weapons, or at least severely limiting their production and stockpiling are necessary means to that end. In general, two types of arenas have been used in pursuit of that goal. Bilateral negotiations between states have usually (when successful) produced arms limitation or control agreements. Multilateral conferences, such as the United Nations Disarmament Conference (with first 18, then 25, and now 30 participants) have been used in pursuit of the more ambitious goal of arms reduction and disarmament.

This simulation recreates some of the major positions and problems that have surrounded arms talks in the recent past. You will play the role of a policy maker in one of our hypothetical nations. Two groups within each nation are represented: the CONTROLLERS, who correspond to those in national governments who are more interested in limiting or even abolishing arms, and the DEFENDERS, the "military-industrial complex" in each nation. In this simulation, the CONTROLLERS in each country are in charge of the governments, but they must come to some understanding with the DEFENDERS so that a unified national position can be presented. Each participant will receive a national scenario which will describe the issues in some detail and suggest initial bargaining positions.

The Director will be responsible for announcing events and the time schedule for the simulation. The Director will also simulate the World Press. Any player may, at any time, submit an item for the press and the Director will announce it, if it is plausible and relevant. The Director will also indicate whether it is an official statement, a rumor or a leak from highly placed sources.

The Countries: YOLO, ZENO, MATRO, and COBO

YOLO and ZENO are the dominant states in the world. Not only are they the most developed, technologically advanced and wealthiest states, but they are also the only ones with large nuclear arsenals. YOLO has built its nuclear capability by concentrating on securing a large number of relatively heavy missiles. ZENO, on the other hand, has developed its arsenal by concentrating on smaller, more accurate warheads and by placing several warheads on each missile.

A balance of terror has existed for some time between YOLO and ZENO, since each is able to credibly threaten to destroy the other if attacked. Spurred by the spiraling costs of weapons, fears of a sneak attack and accidental war, and a pervasive fear that a new technological breakthrough might give the other side a chance to strike first and survive, YOLO and ZENO concluded the famous Pepper agreement five years ago. Basically, Pepper froze each side's forces at current levels and prohibited deployment of an anti-ballistic missile. Now, as the Pepper agreement nears expiration, both sides have agreed to further talks, including MATRO and COBO, and expanding the agenda to include some discussion of a general limitation on nuclear weapons. An added factor in the talks is the consistent rumor that each country is nearing (or has already achieved) a laser-based defensive system.

MATRO is a very large, but poor country. Three years ago, MATRO successfully tested a thermonuclear warhead and has produced enough weapons to equip a fleet of 100 long-range bombers. This makes them a potential threat to both YOLO and ZENO, although current anti-aircraft defense systems in both countries should be able to handle the slow and clumsy MATRO B-13 bombers. However, if MATRO were to develop and deploy ICBMs (Intercontinental Ballistic Missiles) the situation would change dramatically. In the past, MATRO has refused to participate in arms talks with either YOLO or ZENO, charging that such talks simply aimed at freezing the status quo, leaving the "exploiters of the people" firmly in command of the world.

COBO is a relatively small, but highly developed state. Although COBO has not announced any plans for nuclear weapons development, it is well known that their experience with nuclear power generating plants, their technological skills and relatively large military budget would make it possible for COBO to go nuclear very quickly, perhaps producing 150-200 warheads in a year. COBO possesses an Intermediate Range Ballistic Missile (IRBM), nicknamed "YOZEN" with sufficient range to hit either YOLO or ZENO. COBO, like MATRO, lacks all but the most elementary anti-aircraft defense and no missile defense. In the past, COBO has adamantly opposed nuclear weapons, but has lately muted its position.

Current Force Levels

	YOLO	ZENO	MATRO	COBO
ICBM:	1600	1000	—	—
Bombers:[1]	300	900	100	50
Warheads:[2]	1900	7500	100	—
Anti-missile system:	?	?	no	no

1. 150 of YOLO's bombers are old and short range; they cannot hit ZENO. All of ZENO's bombers can reach YOLO. COBO has 300 Yozen missiles with conventional warheads.

2. Each ZENO missile carries three warheads; each bomber carries five.

COBO: Controllers

1. We are faced with one of the most important decisions in the history of our nation: Should we build nuclear weapons? We have long opposed the development or use of these weapons of mass destruction but the changing international situation and what may be a growing threat from MATRO might force us to alter our position. If MATRO decides to build Inter-Continental Ballistic Missiles (ICBMs) it would pose a direct and immediate threat to our survival. If they do not build them, we can easily defend ourselves against their current bomber force. If we decide to build nuclear weapons, we will be forced to divert a substantial amount of money and scientific talent to the project; resources that are badly needed in other areas of the economy.

2. Yet another factor in the nuclear decision is the future behavior of the large powers, YOLO and ZENO. If YOLO and ZENO do not continue the process of negotiating limits on strategic arms, the resulting arms race (which will probably involve MATRO as well) will put even greater pressure on us to compete as well. If the World Disarmament Conference fails, it will be very bad for us, if it results in freezing weapons at current levels we will be under pressure from our defenders to begin building nuclear weapons; if it results in an actual decrease in world military levels it will be best for us.

3. If MATRO continues to act in ways that pose a threat to us, we would seem to have two choices: Either build our own nuclear deterrence force to get YOLO and ZENO to give us solid guarantees of our security against MATRO. We can expect MATRO to advance some proposal for a ban on testing of nuclear weapons. We should regard such an idea suspiciously since we are the only country that has not tested a nuclear weapon and the ones who have the most to lose.

4. In the past, the question of on-site inspection of military forces has been a major source of conflict in arms talks. YOLO and ZENO seem less concerned about it now; inspection of military preparations in MATRO could be highly useful to us, either confirming or disproving the persistent rumors that they are preparing a sneak attack against us.

5. In general, we ought to consider pursuing the following goals:

A. Get the defenders to agree to delay the decision on nuclear weapons until after the conference.

B. Try to steer the conference in the direction of reducing arms stockpiles rather than merely freezing current levels.

C. Avoid a test ban, at least for two years.

D. Push for international inspection of strategic military sites, but not to the extent of preventing progress in the conference.

E. We should definitely prepare a resolution for the conference, trying to set the terms of debate and parameters of the discussion.

COBO: Defenders

1. The nation has all but decided to go nuclear. The arrogance and irresponsibility of YOLO and ZENO, coupled with the increasingly serious threat from MATRO make the decision inevitable. But that decision is not enough. We must build and deploy as many warheads as possible if we are going to survive this time of peril. MATRO is clearly going to build missiles; then we will be extremely vulnerable.

2. YOLO and ZENO may not like our decision; they will have to live with it. If they were willing to guarantee our security against MATRO, we might find it possible to slow down the pace of our deployment. We must be sure that the World Disarmanent Conference does not result in merely freezing current levels of weapons for YOLO, ZENO, and MATRO; but leads to a decrease in world stockpiles. Only if this is done can we look forward to a safer world.

3. MATRO is really as much of a problem as the big two. We can expect them to advance proposals for some sort of test ban that would harm only us. We can also expect MATRO, YOLO, and ZENO to be very interested in preventing our acquisition of nuclear weapons. At the same time, we ought to avoid a stalemated conference because that might induce YOLO and ZENO to deal with each other behind our backs, as they did in Pepper. Such deals serve no one's interests.

4. In general, we ought to consider pursuing the following goals:

   A. Get the Controllers to agree to go nuclear now, and do it rapidly.

   B. Seek a ban on upgrading or replacing existing bomber forces (that will help check MATRO).

   C. Avoid a test ban, at least for two years.

   D. Push for international inspection of all militarily-oriented nuclear facilities. The sophistication of our weapons will impress the world and inspection will help insure that MATRO is living up to its pledges. This point could also be used as a bargaining chip since it is not essential to us. We may want to raise it and then drop it in return for a concession on something else.

   E. We should definitely prepare a resolution for the Conference, trying to set the terms of the debate and perimeters of the discussion.

MATRO: Controllers

1. We must, as a matter of the highest priority, encourage YOLO and ZENO to go beyond the phony Pepper deals and agree to reduce their arsenals. We

must make sure that they deal openly and publicly in these matters, rather than sneaking around behind closed doors to make dirty deals behind the backs of the people of the world.

2. COBO persists in seeing our minimal nuclear arsenal as some kind of terrible threat, when it is really designed as a stop-gap measure to give us some protection from YOLO and ZENO. There is little danger that our current level of forces will affect their determination to avoid going nuclear; if we were to develop the "Avenger" ICBM system, it might well trigger their entry into the world nuclear club.

3. If either YOLO or ZENO (or worse, both) develop some kind of effective anti-missile defense system, we will be completely at their mercy. This must not happen.

4. In general, we should think seriously about the following goals:

A. Seek an open arms agreement, openly arrived at, with full participation by all.

B. Seek an absolute prohibition of an anti-missile system for the superpowers (but not necessarily for ourselves or COBO since an effective system would go a long way toward guaranteeing our safety).

C. Avoid any agreement limiting our right to test and develop new scientific discoveries, such as missile guidance systems.

D. We might want to consider the (somewhat risky) possibility of hinting that we are on the verge of deploying an ICBM, then agreeing not to do so, as a way of wringing concessions out of YOLO, ZENO and COBO.

E. We can expect our defenders to advocate an immediate decision to build and deploy ICBMs and drastically increase our arsenal. This is fine for them to say, since they do not have to deal with the national budget and feed the people. We must resist any final decision.

F. Seek a world-wide test ban treaty, prohibiting any atmospheric nuclear testing. This will effectively prevent COBO from developing significant warheads.

MATRO: Defenders

1. The People's Revolutionary Army is charged with the sacred duty of preserving and extending the revolution. To do this we must increase our national security in the face of constant threats from YOLO and ZENO. The so-called World Disarmament Conference is a fraud; it will fail. Because the Conference will fail, we must be especially alert for signs that YOLO and ZENO are colluding behind closed doors and in secret to cement their domination of the world.

2. COBO persists in pretending that we somehow threaten them. Clearly the militarists of COBO are using our defensive forces for their own corrupt purposes and have already decided to develop nuclear weapons to be used against us. We must therefore proceed immediately to finish the work on the "Avenger" ICBM system within one month and begin deployment within three months. Our own controllers may require some persuasion on this point.

3. If either YOLO or ZENO (or worse, both) develop an effective anti-missile defense system, we are at their mercy (such as it is). This must not happen and must be prevented at the World Disarmament Conference.

4. In general, we should think seriously about these goals:

   A. Seek an open arms agreement, openly arrived at, with full participation by all.

   B. Seek an absolute prohibition of an anti-missile defense for YOLO and ZENO but do not agree to prohibit one for us—it is simply a matter of redressing a grossly unfair balance and defending ourselves.

   C. Avoid any restrictions on our right to test and develop strictly defensive weapons. The "Avenger" is strictly defensive, since it is purely a deterrent device and we will never strike first.

   D. We must get our controllers to approve a crash program for the "Avenger" system.

   E. Seek a test ban treaty that will prohibit atmospheric testing. We are at a stage in development where necessary tests can be conducted underground; COBO is not.

YOLO: Controllers

1. The gravest danger lies in failure to reach agreement with ZENO. The likelihood of either side achieving a usable superiority is nil; we are safe from them and they are safe from us, UNLESS we fail to reach new agreements and charge headlong into a new arms race.

2. ICBMs (the missiles) are the key; we can ignore the ZENO bomber force to some extent because we have ample anti-aircraft defenses and no more than 20 percent of an attacking force could ever get through. This means we have a definite superiority in delivery vehicles and compensates us nicely for their larger supply of warheads. (Actually, the number of warheads is of secondary importance, delivery vehicles are the primary items.)

3. We are on the brink of developing an anti-missile capability, based on laser beams. This is a legitimate development; it is not a violation of Pepper. The Research and Development phase is nearing completion and we will have to

decide, as a country, whether we can afford to let things ride (continuing work on R&D but not moving toward deployment), whether we should accelerate the program slightly to complete R&D and permit us to deploy rapidly if we so choose, or whether we should rush the program to completion by deploying as quickly as possible.

4. In general, we should think seriously about the following goals:

A. Seek an agreement with ZENO that continues the process of negotiated limits on weapons. We have a wide margin of error at this time and don't have to be paranoid about slight differences in delivery systems or warheads.

B. If we can't reach an agreement on equality, we ought to focus on preserving our superiority in missiles and be willing to allow ZENO some edge in warheads. Bombers are somewhat irrelevant.

C. We ought to avoid deploying a Laser Missile Defense (LMD) unless ZENO does it first. Note that it is unclear whether they have a system nearly ready or not.

D. We might want to consider the possibility of revealing exactly where we are no LMD to encourage ZENO to cooperate.

E. WE MUST CONTROL THE NEGOTIATING TEAM FOR SESSION 2 OF THIS GAME.

F. We can expect pressure from the defenders for a hard line with ZENO and/or demands for some new weapons systems and be prepared to resist.

G. Since there is a real danger that the World Disarmament Conference will degenerate into squabbling, it may be wise to begin planning for private talks with ZENO, leading to an extension of Pepper.

YOLO: Defenders

1. The gravest danger lies in the number of warheads that ZENO possesses. They outgun us by better than 3:1 which means that they may be tempted to try to take out our missiles with some of their warheads and then blackmail us. Any agreement must take this imbalance into account and rectify it.

2. There is also a disproportion in delivery vehicles. Past agreements centered only on missiles, freezing us at 1600 and them at 1000. BUT our willingness to talk only about missiles has enabled them to build a massive bomber force, giving ZENO actual superiority in delivery vehicles, as well as warheads. (Note that their 1000 missiles + 900 bombers = 1900 vehicles while our 1600 missiles and only 150 bombers that can be used against them = 1750 vehicles.)

3. We are at the very brink of securing an anti-missile capability, based on laser

beams. This is a legitimate development; it is not a violation of Pepper. The Research and Development phase is nearing completion and we will have to decide, as a country, whether we can afford to let things ride (thus leaving us really vulnerable if it is true that ZENO is also close to a breakthrough), whether we should accelerate the program slightly to complete R&D and allow us to deploy quickly, or whether we should go ahead now, accelerate the program and deploy immediately.

4. COBO and MATRO are insignificant. The only real danger they pose is to our own controllers, who may wish to baby them by making concessions. Neither COBO nor MATRO can possibly ever match us in power, and they will certainly not be stupid enough to try. Especially as we move to deploy the LMD, their puny threats will become laughable. We must, however, beware of ZENO's attempts to play up to COBO and MATRO and score propaganda points with them that may affect our vital interests elsewhere in the world.

5. In general, we should think seriously about the following goals:

A. Seek an agreement with ZENO that gives us equality in warheads.

B. Failing that, seek an agreement that gives us superiority in delivery vehicles to compensate for inferiority in warheads.

C. Seek a national commitment to announce deployment of our Laser Missile Defense (LMD) to protect us against a ZENO advantage or, if they don't yet have it, as a bargaining chip to get concessions from them on other issues.

D. If we can't get C, then we must have at least the commitment to accelerate the LMD program slightly to complete the R&D phase.

E. We should also think seriously about the possibility of getting an entirely new weapons system, one not covered by the details of a Pepper agreement, to redress any imbalance that comes out of the negotiations. (If worst comes to worst, we might have to agree with a national strategy for Pepper that leaves us behind in warheads and delivery systems, as we are now, and in exchange get a commitment for a new program.)

F. WE MUST HAVE AT LEAST ONE REPRESENTATIVE ON THE NEGOTIATING TEAM FOR SESSION 2 OF THIS GAME.

G. Since the World Disarmament Conference will undoubtedly degenerate into petty bickering and foolishness, we should immediately approach ZENO with an offer of secret, bilateral talks.

ZENO: Controllers

1. The gravest danger lies in failure to reach an agreement with YOLO. The likelihood of either side achieving a usable superiority is nil; we are safe from them and they are safe from us, UNLESS we fail to reach new agreements and charge headlong into a new arms race.

2. Warheads are the key. We can ignore the YOLO bomber force to some extent because we have ample anti-aircraft defenses and no more than 20 percent of an attacking force could ever get through. This means we have a definite superiority in warheads and compensates us nicely for their larger supply of delivery vehicles. (Actually, the number of delivery vehicles is of secondary importance, warheads are the primary items.)

3. We are on the brink of developing an anti-missile capability, based on laser beams. This is a legitimate development; it is not a violation of Pepper. The research and development phase is nearing completion and we will have to decide, as a country, whether we can afford to let things ride (continuing work on R&D but not moving toward deployment), whether we should accelerate the program slightly to complete R&D and permit us to deploy rapidly if we so choose, or whether we should rush the program to completion by deploying as quickly as possible.

4. COBO and MATRO are secondary problems. We should strive to point out the utter futility of their trying to compete with us and YOLO and get them to freeze their forces where they are. We must treat them with some caution, though, because YOLO will undoubtedly attempt to score propaganda points with them. We must also be somewhat cautious about their delicate self-images since a too heavy-handed approach could conceivably provoke them into an arms race.

5. In general, we should think seriously about the following goals:

A. Seek an agreement with YOLO that continues the process of negotiated limits on weapons. We have a wide margin of error at this time and don't have to be paranoid about slight differences in warheads or delivery systems.

B. If we can't reach an agreement on equality, we ought to focus on preserving our superiority in warheads and allow YOLO some edge in missiles. Bombers are somewhat irrelevant.

C. We ought to avoid deploying a Laser Missile Defense (LMD) unless YOLO does it first. Note that it is unclear whether they have a system nearly ready or not.

D. We might want to consider the possibility of revealing exactly where we are on LMD to encourage YOLO to cooperate.

E. WE MUST CONTROL THE NEGOTIATING TEAM FOR SESSION 2 OF THIS GAME.

F. We can expect pressure from the defenders for a hard line with YOLO and/or demands for some new weapons systems and be prepared to resist.

G. Since there is a real danger that the World Disarmament Conference will degenerate into squabbling, it may be wise to begin planning for private talks with YOLO, leading to an extension of Pepper.

ZENO: Defenders

1. The gravest danger lies in the number of delivery vehicles YOLO possesses. They outgun us by better than 1½:1 which means they may be tempted to take out our missiles with some of their warheads and blackmail us with the rest. Any agreement must take this imbalance into account and rectify it.

2. There is also a serious problem with the number of warheads, despite what the figures seem to say. Note that while we have more warheads, they don't do us much good if we have fewer delivery vehicles, which are vulnerable to sneak attack. Disregard of this obvious problem has led to the present difficult situation under Pepper.

3. We are on the brink of an anti-missile capability, based on laser technology. Since it does not use missiles, it is not in violation of the earlier agreements. We have to decide whether we wish to let the project die now, or whether we wish to accelerate the pace slightly to complete the Research and Development phase and be prepared for deployment, or whether we should go ahead now and begin deployment. We can assume that YOLO will deploy some kind of anti-missile system as soon as they get it. Can we afford to be second?

4. COBO and MATRO are potentially dangerous. If either or both countries were to deploy a significant force, it would seriously complicate our situation and make both the LMD and an entirely new generation of weapons systems imperative for national survival. At best, we should try to get them to agree to a strictly limited deployment. To achieve this, it may be necessary to make some minor concessions to them during the talks.

5. In general, we should think most seriously about the following goals:

   A. Seek an agreement with YOLO that gives us equality in delivery vehicles.

   B. Failing that, seek an agreement that gives us superiority in warheads to compensate for inferiority in delivery vehicles.

   C. Seek a national commitment to announce deployment of our Laser Missile Defense (LMD) to protect us against a YOLO advantage or, if they don't have it yet, as a bargaining chip to get concessions from them on other issues.
   D. If we can't get C, then we must have at least the commitment to accelerate the LMD program slightly, to complete the R&D phase.

   E. We should also think seriously about the possibility of getting an entirely new weapons system, one not covered by the details of a Pepper agreement, to redress any imbalance that comes out of the negotiations. (If worst comes to worst, we might have to agree with a national strategy for Pepper that leaves us behind in delivery systems, and in exchange get a commitment for a new program.)

F. WE MUST HAVE AT LEAST ONE REPRESENTATIVE ON THE NEGOTIATING TEAM FOR SESSION 2 OF THIS GAME.

G. If the World Disarmament Conference degenerates into petty bickering, it may be necessary to deal with YOLO bilaterally, lest Pepper expire and leave us with nothing.

Conference Diplomacy

JoAnn F. Aviel
San Francisco State University

Rather than a single simulation, this is a framework which can be applied to a variety of topics in any college level course dealing with foreign policy questions. The primary objective of the simulation is to analyze and improve understanding of the complex processes involved in foreign policy decision-making and negotiations. Simulations have been conducted dealing with problems of international energy, food, commodity, disarmament, the New Economic Order, the Middle East and the law of the sea. The number of students has varied from eight to 35. The actual conduct of the simulation takes a minimum of two class sessions. The first session is an agenda conference in order to agree on the specific topics which will be discussed at the subsequent substantive or summit conference. The summit conference can take from one to three sessions with either the participants or the instructor determining the limit. It is usually helpful to provide a session in between the two conferences in order for participants to further prepare their country positions and to negotiate informally with each other. Such a session before the agenda conference can also be helpful but is not necessary. It is desirable to have a large room or several small ones available for simultaneous informal negotiations. Each country should have a placard and a designated space for the "home office."

Two different formats have been used for assigning roles. In one each student represents a different country and is that country's delegate to both the agenda and summit conferences. This format has the advantage of providing a wide number of countries to participate in the conferences. In the other format each country is represented by a team including a minimum of two members—the foreign minister and the head of government, with additional members such as ministers of defense, economy, agriculture, or energy added depending on class size and the topic of the conference. This format has the advantage of providing a better understanding of the problems involved in deciding on a common policy between members of a single government but with often conflicting interests. Before the conferences, students prepare a position paper with topics varying somewhat in each format.

In the first format each student prepares a paper of approximately ten pages describing background relevant to the country and the problem to be discussed at the conferences. The instructor needs to introduce the problem and provide bibliographic information. For a simulation dealing with international food and fuel problems, students had to supply data on the general state of their country's economy, and the food and fuel the country imported and exported (if any) and from whom. They analyzed how decisions were made regarding food and fuel policy in their country and the principal problems which it faced. They researched what positions governments had taken at recent international conferences and predicted the likely positions which would be taken in the future in preparing their strategy for the simulated conferences.

In the other format each student is responsible for preparing a position paper based on their individual roles as Ministers in charge of Foreign Affairs, Material Production, Human Development, Agriculture or Energy. The paper includes a statement of the problem with a list of the goals or objectives which the minister feels should be realized at the conference, ranked in order of priority. Next the minister must identify alternative national policies or options and analyze the costs and benefits of each before recommending a policy which should focus on specific proposals which their country might make at the conference. In this last section students are asked to suggest what tactics and arguments should be used or avoided as their country deals with the others and which countries scheduled to attend the conference may be possible allies or opponents under particular circumstances. The paper is approximately five pages, not counting any draft proposals which may be attached as appendices. The paper of the student who represents the Head of Government is due after the others and should make use of the information supplied by the ministers. The various recommended policies contained in the ministry position papers can be considered as alternative national policies with the recommended policy to be that which the Head of Government intends to pursue at the summit conference.

If the instructor wishes to provide the students with an opportunity for more in-depth analysis, students can be divided into country teams early in the class session. Students can first prepare a detailed background paper, with each student researching and answering questions supplied by the instructor dealing with different aspects of the assigned country, i.e., political system, economic system, foreign and defense system, and human development system, so that students develop expertise in different areas. Each team can then prepare an oral background briefing supplemented with audio-visual materials. Each student can be responsible for a five-minute presentation, after which a question and answer session of approximately half an hour can follow. This provides the students with an opportunity to demonstrate their expertise and to learn about each other's countries prior to the simulation.

Rules of procedure for the conferences are kept relatively simple. Each conference opens with short speeches outlining each country's position. Any delegate is permitted to request a suspension of the formal session for a designated period of time to permit informal negotiations. Decisions on this and other procedural matters, as well as all decisions taken at the agenda conference, are by a simple majority. Decisions at the summit conference have usually been taken by a qualified majority. The instructor may want to experiment with other rules or even have the students decide on what should be required for the summit conference at the agenda conference, although this usually takes a great deal of time. At the agenda conference topics should be presented in as detailed a format as possible and the conference must decide the order of priority of items to be discussed at the summit conference. This is important since many summit conferences do not have time to consider all the items proposed. Heads of government should come prepared with detailed proposals on which the delegates can vote and if possible have consulted with likely allies prior to the conference. These proposals are duplicated and distributed to other delegates.

The instructor has usually chaired the conferences in the role of an impartial representative of the United Nations Secretariat. At times more detailed rules of procedure based on those used in model United Nations sessions have been used, but they have usually not proved necessary. During the informal negotiation phases all communication between and among country teams should be in written form only, except when prior written agreement has been given to face-to-face meetings at a scheduled time and place. During this time the instructor or an assistant has acted as international courier. During the formal conference proceedings the voting delegate may confer only in writing with other members of the country team.

As in most simulations the debriefing session following the conferences is most important for realizing instructional objectives. Although an evaluation paper may be required, the usual procedure has been for each student to prepare a short speech for this session including the following points: (1) identification of country objectives which were realized at the conference; (2) description of the part the student played in realizing the objectives; (3) identification of objectives which were not reached and analysis of why efforts failed; and (4) an analysis of the problems of conference decision-making and negotiation. Discussions at these debriefing sessions have often become quite heated as students question each other on strategies employed and decisions taken. The instructor needs to provide material based on actual conferences to enable students to make comparisons with what took place in their simulated conferences. Students usually comment on the frustrations and complexities of international negotiations and their improved understanding of foreign policy decision-making in general, and the particular problem with which they were involved carry over into subsequent course work.

Three International Politics Simulations

J. E. Lawyer
Bethel College

For the past two years I have used a simplified simulation of international conferences in my "World Politics" course with good results. We normally hold three such simulations per term, each one attempting to deal with a different major international issue (nuclear terrorism, law of the sea, energy policy, etc.) and a different institutional setting (an ad hoc international conference, the Governing Body of a UN Specialized Agency, and the UN General Assembly). Students have reacted positively to the experience by getting deeply into the subject material in each issue, by a heightened interest in course material presented in the more conventionally taught intervals between conferences, and in gaining a new appreciation for the irrational and often counterproductive dynamics of the international scene. While I have found that the knowledge and insights students gain in the course of a three-conference series is cumulative, there is no reason why an instructor could not use any one of them alone to advantage. As always, flexibility and adaptability are the keynotes of a successful simulation experience.

For the first conference, players are divided into eight four-person national delegations representing a cross-cut of governments (typically, Brazil, the FRG, Iran, Japan, Nigeria, the PRC, the USSR, and the U.S.). Each delegation has four ministerial positions to divide up as it wishes.[1] While ministerial assignments may change within the delegation from conference to conference, each player remains a member of the same "country team" for all three conferences.

Each delegation is responsible for researching, writing, presenting and defending its national position in response to the conference agenda, which is handed out at the start of the week before. The agenda contains four items,[2] so each member of the delegation becomes something of a specialist in his area, but must also have a broad enough understanding of all factors to ensure that the delegation's position is consistent over the whole range of issues (which does not always happen, either in the exercise or in real life).

To ensure that all participants have done their preparation, copies of these position papers are collected at the opening session of each conference. In the ensuing class time, each delegation has the floor for approximately 15 minutes. In that period they present their position on each of the four agenda items, and field comments and questions from other delegates. If class size requires, the

---

[1] Law of the Sea Conference: Foreign Minister; Defense Minister; Minister of Resources and Economic Development; Fisheries Commissioner. Energy Conference: Foreign Minister; Petroleum Minister (LDCs) or Energy Minister (DCs); Finance Minister; Director of Foreign Assistance (DCs) or Minister of National Development (LDCs). Non-Proliferation Conference: Foreign Minister; Defense Minister; Energy Minister (DCs) or Minister of National Development (LDCs); Atomic Energy Commissioner.

[2] Law of the Sea Conference: fishing rights and marine research; the delimitation of territorial waters and international straits; a regime to govern the 200-mile economic zone; a regime for the deep seabed and the exploitation of its mineral wealth. Energy Conference: price and quantity of oil brought to market; how to finance world oil purchases/sales; assistance to the LDCs; political aspects of the oil situation. Non-Proliferation Conference: Measures to limit the spread of nuclear weaponry; nuclear testing and disarmament proposals; exports of nuclear materials and technologies for peaceful purposes; safeguards and international enforcement machinery).

class could be broken down to as few as six three-person teams (with parallel reduction in agenda items), or can be expanded upwards to a maximum of about 40 participants. Extra people can serve as conference chairpersons or members of the international secretariat, responsible for preparing, presenting and defending a "best-interests-of-the-world-community" position.

One week of normal class time (three one-hour sessions, or two longer periods) is about the right amount of time for an eight-delegation conference. It generally takes more than one class period for students to become familiar with the activity, and interest begins to wane if a conference lasts beyond a week. At the same time, I have had good results with holding up to three one-week conferences a term, roughly the last week of each month, with new subject matter and some variations in procedure.

In the second conference, players caucus with their counterparts from other delegations (i.e., all the Finance Ministers meeting together) and then rejoin the other ministers making up their own national delegation, who have meanwhile been off caucasing with *their* counterparts, often reaching quite different approaches to the issues. The instructor drifts inconspicuously from one group to another to keep abreast of developments. The final hour is then given to an open meeting of each of the four caucuses (15 minutes each), in which the delegates attempt to reconcile the new instructions received while meeting together as a national delegation with the on-going thrust of the meeting with their fellow Ministers of Whatever from other governments.

In the third and final conference, near the end of the term, I have the groups meet in two bloc caucuses, developed countries in one, LDCs in the other, to draw up resolutions and trade votes. Since the conference is structured so that there will be four countries in each caucus, if any one country can be wooed away from its "natural" partners by the other coalition, the larger bloc can carry the conference. For the first part of this week's activity, delegations alternate between private and bloc sessions. The final hour is devoted to a plenary where each delegation may offer one resolution. I have found it works best to consider these by roll call vote, in rotating alphabetical order by country (as at the UN itself), in order to avert the pandemonium of a voice vote. Usually by this time feelings are running high, and as deals can be made and unmade in a matter of minutes, the inherent proclivity to disorder must be guarded against. Generally, holding a vote tends to focus student interest too much on winning or losing, at the expense of getting into the substantive issues involved; for that reason, this is the only vote taken in all three conferences.

By pacing conferences in this way, students build their familiarity with the conference simulation format. They also become better acquainted with their country's position, interests, and constraints. The new material and procedures, and the change from more conventional class sessions, suffices to keep interest high.

Only minimal physical facilities are needed beyond normal class require-ments. The main requirement is for a fairly large classroom, with movable furniture. It is important to have the delegates of each country sit together, and to have some sort of public space separating the presenting delegation from the other members of the conference. Hallways and empty classrooms can be used for national delegation meetings, if desired. Any additional equipment (flags, national dress, nameplates, etc.) can enrich the setting and further stimulate student interest, but care should be taken as this aspect of things can easily get out of hand.

Students have the week prior to each conference to research their national position papers on the agenda items outside of class, with no other assignments that week. The instructor may provide folders of relevant newsclips, articles, Department of State publications, or other such materials, or simply leave the research to the students, depending on library resources, level of student capabilities, etc. During the week of the conference itself I assign normal reading related to the following week, since the bulk of the conference activity is now taking place during the class periods. Students have welcomed an option to rewrite their position papers over the weekend following the first conference, as it is hard for a novice to anticipate what a good paper would look like before having gone through the experience. I make it clear, however, that that option will not be extended after other conferences, to discourage freeloading on those who have more conscientiously prepared for the conference sessions.

Evaluation consists of grading the position papers. Since these are short (not more than three pages, double spaced), typed, and requested in outline or talking-paper format for easier use and revision during the give-and-take of the conference itself, I have found they can be evaluated quite quickly. An added help is that, with the conference carrying itself for the week, papers can be graded in the time normally devoted to lesson preparation. Other instructors may wish to give credit for oral presentation and conference participation, but I have found it distracting to try to evaluate individuals at the same time that I am keeping track of the pulse of the conference as a whole.

Who Gets What, When and How?

Donald Ostrom
Gustavus Adolphus College

I have used "Who Gets What, When and How" in introductory U.S. Government classes, but it could be adapted to other courses such as urban politics or state politics.* Unlike most simulations, "Who Gets What, When and

---

*The original inspiration for my use of simple simulation in the classroom was a 1974 APSA short course given by William Coplin and Michael O'Leary, and "The Good Society Exercise" of the International Relations Program of Syracuse University provided my first model. Over the years I have revamped the simulation into its present form for my U.S. Government classes.

How" is an introduction to the subject, rather than a culmination of a course or unit. The simulation is used early in the semester, usually in the first week. There is no reading preparation needed by the students to participate in the simulation.

"Who Gets What, When and How" is used to stimulate students in the introductory course to think about the relationship between various have and have-not groups in the society, the interaction of political and economic power, and the means used to preserve or alter the status quo. The simulation can bring home to students, sometimes even in an emotional way, what it is like to be ignored by other groups in the society because they possess only "4 points" of economic strength, or the different outcomes that are possible because of superior strength, strategic analysis, or negotiation skill and energy. I then refer to the experiences of the simulation in lectures and discussions later in the semester.

"Who Gets What, When and How" is designed to be played in one class period of 50 minutes. But this means the negotiations and other discussions are rushed, and the simulation could well be adapted to two hours if the instructor can conveniently assemble the students for the longer time period. The economic strength and political strength of the various groups can also be altered, depending on the instructor's assessment of the relative influence of various groups in the society. Except for Government, I have labeled the groups with rather non-descriptive titles (A, B, C, etc.); other, more colorful titles could label groups Chicago Economic Establishment, Chicago Democrats, Downstate Republicans, Downstate Residents, Chicago Blacks, Chicago Whites, etc.).

The sample instructions given here are designed to be played by a class of at least 18 and at most 24-30 students. Again, the number can be altered by adding more groups, but I have found it best not to have more than four or five members in a group (group members often learn that it is exciting to be a Representative and run around talking with other Representatives and groups, and much less interesting to "stay home"; but from the standpoint of student morale, there is a need to limit the number of students experiencing the frustration of playing the more boring roles in the society).

The physical facilities needed for the simulation are simple. It can be done in the regular classroom, with different groups meeting in different sections of the room. If the simulation is played in the evening and at greater length, arrangements can be made to use different rooms or faculty offices for each of the groups. Sometimes, for example, I have given the Government team a rather isolated location to observe what political consequences this has. However, given the time limits and the need to keep the simulation interesting, the locations of the teams should in general not be so far apart that communication becomes too difficult.

The preparation by the instructor is limited. I usually give out the instructions the class period before the simulation is to occur. I briefly explain the simulation, and then ask the students to read and try to understand the instructions and bring them to the next class period (but I also have some extra instructions ready at the next class period for the students who have not remembered to bring them). Before the simulation period I post simple signs, magic marker on paper hung up with masking tape, in different locations of the room for the different groups. When the students assemble, I ask for any questions they have about the simulation, and then quickly have them count off (Government, A, B, C, D, E, Government, A, B, etc.) and move to their assigned group location. In the initial strategy session I move around, counseling any groups which appear bewildered and stymied. I also hand out badges for the Representatives (the badges are usually the simple peel-away sticker identification badges possessed in abundance by the school's public relations office; I put the group's name on the badge). The strategy and negotiation sessions then follow, alternating until near the end of the class period.

The end of the class period is saved for the most important part of the simulation, the debriefing. I try to have at least 8-10 minutes for debriefing in a 50-minute simulation, and more than that in a longer simulation. Following are some of the most common questions I ask:

What was your group trying to achieve? Did you succeed? Why or why not?
Which was more interesting, being a Representative, or "staying home"?
Why was so little attention paid to Group E (or D and E)?
Did political skill play a part in the simulation, or was it only a question of power? Which skills were important?
Why did different groups, and different individuals within groups, seem to have different ideas of what should be done in this society?
Does this simulation correspond to reality? Do groups behave this way? How is it different from reality?

I have found it easier to get a discussion going in this debriefing period than in any other classroom situation. The students have insights, and they often express them ardently.

Simulations, like all other teaching techniques, do not achieve uniformly excellent results every time or with every student. But "Who Gets What, When and How" is a low-risk simulation. It requires little preparation by the instructor or students, involves no costly materials, and takes little class time. Even if the simulation would completely flop, only one class period would be wasted. However, it has been my experience after using it a great many times that "Who Gets What, When and How" does stimulate a learning and involvement by the students that in many cases could not occur in any other way.

Instructions

This simulation will be conducted by six groups, consisting of three or more participants each. The six groups are called Government, A, B, C, D, and E. The groups believe in the following *Creed:*

We believe in equal opportunity and equal rights. Nobody should be denied the chance to get ahead and improve their station in life. We admire strength and justice.

Although the Creed is generally believed, not all people believe in all passages with equal fervor. In any case, the rewards of this society, as indicated by the economic and political strength, are not distributed equally. Also, seeking change (or protecting the status quo) can be accomplished more easily by some groups than by others. What happens when there are differences and ambiguities in the principles and practices of a society?

Rewards, Stability, and Change

The relative economic and political influence of each group is indicated in the following table:

Group	Economic Strength	Political Strength
Government	40	5
A	80	3
B	30	3
C	11	2
D	8	2
E	4	2
Total	173	17

Changes, including redistribution of economic and political strength, can be accomplished in two different ways:

Economic action, like political action, can be used to redistribute either groups. The more powerful faction (the one with greater economic strength) wins.

2. *Political Action:* Three or more groups representing at least nine points of political strength can make revisions.

+*conomic action, like political action, can be used to redistribute either economic or political strength.* However, there can be no change in the total of economic strength (173) or political strength (17). No fractions are permitted, nor can any group be reduced below one point of economic strength and one point of political strength. Forms for economic action and political action are printed on the last page of these instructions.

Step by Step Instructions

1. Each of the groups will meet apart from each other.

2. Approximately the first eight minutes of the simulation will be devoted to strategy sessions within groups. Each group should examine the Creed (above), and in light of the Creed discuss the group's goals. Does the group wish to maintain the status quo? Does it seek change? What kind of change? Whether the status quo or change is preferred, *how* is the goal to be achieved?

Recognize that no group under the initial distribution of economic and political strength can prevail by itself against all others. What kind of persuasion, argument, threat, or other technique can be used to attain the group's goal?

3. Each of the groups should choose representatives for the negotiation session to follow. Each group with three members should choose one representative; groups with four or more members should choose two representatives.

4. Following the strategy session, a five-minute negotiation session will occur. The Representatives of each group are allowed to travel to other groups to discuss changes in the society, and attempt to persuade other groups to take economic or political action. There will be alternating five-minute negotiation and strategy sessions, signaled by the instructor, until the end of the simulation.

5. Change resulting from political action goes into effect as soon as announced by the instructor. In order for this to occur, the instructor must receive a political action form signed by all members of teams representing at least nine points of political strength.

6. Economic actions do not go into effect until three minutes after the instructor announces that he has received an economic action form and states the nature of the change. During these three minutes counter-actions can occur, if the necessary signatures are gathered. The group(s) with the greater economic strength will prevail; the instructor will announce the result.

7. After changes have occurred, the new levels of strength will be in effect. These levels can also, of course, be changed by subsequent economic or political action.

8. Near the end of the period, following the last negotiation session, there will be a discussion of the simulation. What were each of the groups trying to achieve? Which were successful? Why? How did this simulation depart from reality? How did it correspond to reality?

Exercises in Tacit Coordination*

Seth Thompson
Loyola Marymount University

I

Subject: These exercises focus on tacit coordination: the ability of people to cooperate in the absence of any explicit communication.

Courses: Can be used in any course at almost any level where the concept is appropriate. Has been used in a freshman-level introductory course and a senior-level International Politics course.

Players: There are no specific roles. Students are divided into pairs for each exercise. If there are an odd number of students, the instructor can join to make the final pair (the instructor's knowledge of the "solution" has a minimal impact on the exercise). It may be desirable, but not necessary, to change the pairing for each exercise. There is an obvious minimum of two students; there is no maximum and the exercises should work well even in very large classes.

Time: Each exercise can be completed in less than five minutes; total time invested will be a function of how much discussion the instructor wishes to allow after each exercise. All four exercises, with some discussion, can be easily completed in one 50-minute class session or extended to an additional session.

Materials: The only essential requirement is that each student have access to the map for Exercise 1. The instructions for each exercise can be given verbally or duplicated and passed out. If that is done, students should not receive the instructions for more than one exercise at a time.

II

These exercises focus on the possibilities and limitations of cooperative behavior in the absence of direct communication and structured rules for coordinating behavior. The first three revolve around the presence of some unique feature in a situation (physical structures in exercise one and two, the common notion of a 50-50 split as "fair" in exercise three) and the ability of individuals to predict the behavior of their partners. Exercise four complicates matters by introducing a cultural variable with the intent of redefining what is obvious or commonsensical.

---

*The concept of tacit coordination and the first three exercises are adopted from Thomas Schelling, *The Strategy of Conflict,* Harvard University Press, 1963, pp. 54-56.

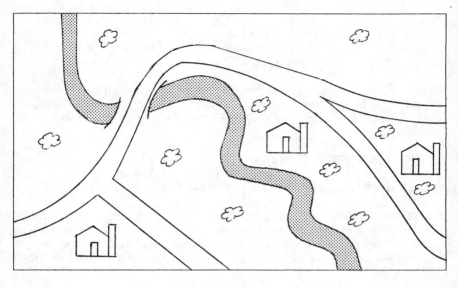

Map Key:

= house   = bush   = river   = road   = bridge

EXERCISE 1: INSTRUCTIONS

1. Divide students into pairs who will play together. COMMUNICATION OF ANY SORT BETWEEN STUDENTS IS PROHIBITED. Either reproduce the map on a chalkboard or give a copy to each student.

2. Each student locates him or herself at any point on the map, without communicating that location to anyone else.

3. Each pair of students is told by the director, "The area you are in is deserted (the houses are vacant). One of you has a short wave radio that can be used to call for help but no batteries for it.

   The other member of the pair has the batteries. Thus, you need to find each other. Where do you go to find your partner?"

4. Once each person has decided where to go, members of each pair announce to their partners where they are.

Discussion

1. How many pairs managed to meet at the same place? (Almost always successful pairs will end up at the bridge.)

2. What was it about the bridge that made it a likely meeting spot? (For most people the bridge stands out as an "obvious" solution because it is unique; if there were two bridges and only one house the house would emerge as the solution.)

EXERCISE 2: INSTRUCTIONS

1. Students remain in pairs and communication is not allowed.

2. Director announces to each pair, "You and your partner agree to meet on campus on a particular day. However, you forgot to agree on where you would meet and when you would meet. Tomorrow is the day of the meeting. Where do you go and when do you show up to give yourself the best chance of meeting?"

3. Once players have decided individually where and when they will show up, they compare notes.

Discussion

1. How many pairs managed to meet? Where and when?

2. This exercise will either recreate the dynamics of Exercise 1 or it will produce far fewer solutions, depending on the nature of the particular campus. Many people will be able to coordinate on the time of the meeting (noon is a common choice) but some campuses lack a single central location or focal point and it may prove almost impossible for people to agree on location.

EXERCISE 3: INSTRUCTIONS

1. Students remain in pairs without communication.

2. Students are told, "You and your partner jointly own a piece of property. The tax bill for your property is $100 and is due now. Since you cannot communicate with your partner, each of you will have to decide how much or how little of the joint bill you will pay. If the total of your payments is $100, well and good. If the total of your payments is less than $100, the tax collector will assess a fine of an additional $100. If the total of your payment is more than $100, the tax collector will accept it as a voluntary contribution and keep it. How much of the $100 do you pay?"

3. Once each student has decided on how much she/he will pay, they compare notes.

Discussion

1. Most people will agree on a 50-50 split and each will pay $50.

2. Unlike the first two exercises, there is an additional element in this case: players share a common interest in paying exactly $100 as a total tax but they also have (presumptively) an individual interest in paying as little in taxes as possible. There is the potential for a clash between self-interest and group (or pair) interests.

EXERCISE 4: INSTRUCTIONS

1. Instructions are the same as Exercise 3 EXCEPT for the addition of this statement: "Forget, for the moment, that you are American college students and assume that you live in a different culture, one that values generosity very highly. In fact, in your culture a reputation for generosity is more important than wealth or knowledge in giving a man or woman status in the community. With this in mind, how much of the joint tax bill do you offer to pay?"

2. Once each student has decided how much to pay, they compare notes.

Discussion

1. If students take the additional instructions seriously, a 50-50 split is much less likely to emerge and most pairs will overpay.

2. The first three exercises hinge on people's ability to find "obvious" or "common sense" solutions. This exercise allows for discussion of the extent to which "common sense" of the "obvious" are culturally determined. The discussion might explore the difficulties this phenomenon poses for bargaining or cooperation between nations or groups within nations that reflect cultural assumptions.

Identifying Variables

Roberta Ann Johnson
University of California, Santa Cruz (visiting)

Goals: Cognitive

1. To teach students how to identify and label variables comfortably.

2. To teach students to question social scientists' claims of correlation in an organized and analytic fashion.

3. To develop the confidence necessary to work with setups in an imaginative and enthusiastic and autonomous way.

Behavioral

1. To create a more relaxed classroom atmosphere.

2. To create a situation where students teach each other.

The Assignment: Used in conjunction with Morris Rosenberg's *The Logic of Survey Analysis* (Basic Books, New York, 1968) (especially Chapter 3, "Intervening and Antecedent Variables," and Chapter 4, "Suppressor and Distorter Variables").

The Class: Designed for an introductory lower division political analysis or research course.

Requirements: The class was divided into groups of four or five each. The simulation requires at least two groups. Time: eight minutes minimum for the groups to work out the problem; five minutes minimum for each group to present solution. The simulation requires a regular classroom with movable chairs and enough room between groups that they don't interfere with each other.

The Game: After spending one or two class meetings explaining what an hypothesis is, what a variable is, and after defining independent, dependent, antecedent, intervening and suppressor variables and illustrating with many examples, the class is ready for the game.

I divide them into groups of four in the least disruptive way, grouping where they sit. If the class sits in a segregated way, segregated by gender, race or intelligent participation (sometimes the "sleepers" sit in the back), you might want to group them by alphabetized name or using numbers.

The game is about to start.

In a container, a box, or hat, I have placed a number of strips of folded paper, on each is written an hypothesis. This creates surprise and a game atmosphere. Someone in each group picks a paper from the container. The following are some of the hypotheses I have used:

Female students at San Francisco State get better grades than male students.
At San Francisco State, math majors have fewest dates.
Students within a 10-mile radius of school get better grades than those outside the radius.
At San Francisco State, psychology majors have more personal problems than other majors.

At San Francisco State, political science majors are more likely to be placed in jobs, graduate and professional schools than other majors.

The groups have eight minutes to identify the dependent and independent variables and to suggest a possible antecedent, intervening and suppressor variable. There is lots of enthusiastic talking as they label and prepare. Each group decides who writes and who will report for the group. Peer group pressure is an incentive for participation within the group and also for an intelligent presentation to the class. Then, each group makes its five-minute presentation.

When they report, I write what they say on the blackboard, using arrows, showing everyone, visually, what the relationships are they are describing.

Evaluation of Goals

Cognitive. In terms of learning, the exercise forces students to label, and apply new terms. By applying them, they will remember them longer. They become comfortable using the terms and they become much more confident using packaged setups, deciding on their own hypotheses and what to control for, which is what this exercise is really designed to prepare them for.

Most important, students learn to be suspicious—suspicious of hypotheses that stop short of controlling for the "hidden" variables, the intervening or antecedent factors that might be the real explanation for claimed correlation. They are much more confident to critique the claims of political science.

Behavioral. The major purpose of the game is, of course, cognitive but it also has a behavioral payoff. Students working together break down the formality of the classroom and their enthusiasm is infectious—pours into and changes the class atmosphere and makes the class more relaxed. Also the students have experience teaching each other which makes them more confident and independent—a healthy space for budding social scientists to be in.